To Pamela,

Thank you for your
wonderful support!
Keep berning brightly :)

All the best,

P.H.

Bernie On!

Chicago to Philly on foot for Bernie Sanders
and the Political Revolution

Bernhard Forcher

Cover designed and created by Rodrigo Villacorta

Cover photo by Alice Sharpe

For true Democracy

Preface

This book and the journey it describes were inspired by Senator Bernie Sanders and the people who gave - quite literally - their last dime to support him. It has nothing to do with Democrats vs. Republicans - I'm not interested in being pro one or contra the other. Too much time, energy and money has already gone into that never-ending strife, which is - in my opinion - a distraction to the American public more than anything else. I know some will disagree in this matter, and so I want the reader to know what not to expect.

Here's what to expect instead: Bernie Sanders is a hero in my eyes. More than that, I believe wholeheartedly that he is a prophet, at least in the way I understand the meaning of the word *prophet*: a man or a woman who brings Truth to the world in a time when Truth has been forgotten. Who reminds humankind of its most essential values, without which it cannot continue on a path of prosperity, harmony, peaceful coexistence and spiritual growth. In addition, the reader will find that I sometimes express strong, possibly unfavorable opinions in regards to other political figures, who played a crucial part during the 2016 Democratic primary. They are my opinions - nothing more and nothing less - and the reader is of course entitled to their own.

The photographs in this book are meant to be viewed in color, but had to be printed in black & white in order to avoid unreasonably high costs. If you can, please look up the originals for a more enjoyable reading experience: *fb.me/bernieforbernie*

Bernie Sanders rattled millions of us out of our sleep. If you were one of them, you know what I'm talking about. If you were on the other team(s) during the 2016 primary elections, maybe you've since opened up to Bernie's message, which - as he himself had reminded us at every opportunity - had nothing to do with him at the end of the day: he was just the messenger. And if you weren't involved at all, if you paid no mind back then for one of ten million reasons, I hope my story can help you understand how deeply Senator Bernie Sanders shook the foundations of the United States of America we thought to be our reality - and the giant movement he gave birth to...

- Bernhard Forcher

All Is Lost

'...no, no, no, tell me it's not true! He would never do that, I know he wouldn't. So many sacrificed so much, it can't all be for nothing! Please tell me it's not true...'

My thoughts kept spinning in circles like this, but I soon conceded: the unthinkable had happened, and I couldn't make it unhappen.

The *unthinkable* - to clarify - was Senator Bernie Sanders' endorsement of his rival, former Secretary of State Hillary Clinton, during the 2016 Democratic primary. There had been rumors of this possibility for some time now, but I had played them down. It wasn't going to happen, I was certain. And now, on the morning of the 12th of July, it had. Just like that.

I felt empty. I felt nothing. I was far away from my home of Los Angeles, CA. 2,500 miles from my friends, my work, my cats. I thought I might as well just sit here on the side of the road in whatever corner of rural Ohio I was in, with my sun-faded Bernie T-shirt, my taped up shins, stiff knees and swollen ankles, my tar stained Asics running shoes with aching feet stuck inside, my backpack in the grass next to me, and wait for death. Okay, that's not true - I didn't consider waiting for death. I didn't think any such dramatic thoughts. My spirit was crushed by a corrupt political machine, and I was paralyzed from the sudden demise of my purpose: my walk from Chicago to Philadelphia for Bernie Sanders and his supporters.

It was suddenly utterly pointless. Meaningless. Bernie would not be the nominee - not after endorsing his opponent. So what was the point of keeping going? I wasn't even in Pennsylvania yet. I hadn't even put half of the total 734 miles behind me. How could I possibly endure any more of this ordeal of walking 27 miles a day in the blistering summer heat for no reason at all? 'Come home', my friend Ian texted me. 'We miss you, man.' It seemed only logical. None of the thousands of Bernie supporters, who had morally carried me on their shoulders via their encouraging comments, likes and reactions on Facebook - the people I did this whole walk for to begin with, to help them hang in until the convention - would now have anything to draw from it. The convention didn't matter anymore, thus neither did my walk. We were finished - *I* was finished.

I still had 12 miles to go to my resting place for the night. Some motel in Canton, OH. 'I have to get there in any case', I thought. 'There's nothing around here but a few houses and farms every mile or so...'

So I got up. Sounds like a simple enough act, right? Not for me. Not at this point in my journey. *No* physical act was simple anymore: my knees were so stiff, I couldn't sit down or get up without using my arms for support. Which would have been fine, had my wrists not been completely shot from riding on the scooter - my crutch to help heal my injuries - for almost a week now. I moved like a man twice my age. Actually, scratch that. That would make me 74. Bernie was 74, and he would have looked like a high school athlete next to me in this moment. But you get the idea...

I shouldered my backpack. God, it was so heavy. How to continue putting one foot in front of the other when both of them hurt as much as they did? 'Well, at least this will be my last day having to go through this ordeal', I thought in between moaning and groaning from pain and exhaustion. And then... *something* happened. Something I'm still not able to wrap my mind around. Something that turned everything upside down. Something that made giving up a non option. Something I don't know what to call other than *divine intervention*:

As I went through the motions of preparing to head out, I took

2

notice of the property across the street - a charming white house on a large green meadow, nestled within lush trees. Pretty. Like countless places in Ohio. It didn't really stand out in any way, and I would have forgotten all about it five minutes down the road, had my eyes not fallen on the old rusty mailbox sitting on a wooden post in the front yard. I looked more closely at the letters - *the family name* - written on the side of it. I squinted in confusion as my brain pieced them together. '*What* is this sign saying?' a voice in my head inquired, hesitant and unsure if my eyes were playing a trick on me. I walked closer and soon stood there with jaw wide open, mesmerized, staring at the words before me in awe and disbelief...

Inspiration

I have to back up a bit at this point, and walk you through (pun intended) how I had ended up here. A few quick details:

My name is Bernhard Forcher. I was born in 1979, in a small town called Lienz in the mountains of Austria. I grew up in a middle class home with two sisters. My Dad was a teacher, and my Mom raised us and took care of the home. As a teenager Axl Rose was my hero and so I decided I wanted to be a singer. After a few years in a rock band I studied musical theater in Vienna and worked as a stage actor in Austria and Germany quite successfully for three years, before deciding that Film and TV were more my thing, and that I needed to be in the US to really dive into that. So I packed my bags and headed to New York in 2006, and after two and a half years there I finally made my move to the city it was all happening in: Los Angeles.

Things were tough that year. And the year after. There was almost zero chance for a new actor to break into the business during the writers' strike and the SAG (Screen Actors Guild) strike. And it didn't end there: the financial crash in 2008 still had everyone clinging to their jobs like their lives depended on it - which they probably did - and I couldn't even get a job at Subway. And I tried - at many locations. Eventually Starbucks gave me a shot and I earned my stripes as a barista/cleaning personnel for thirteen months before deciding I couldn't do what I came here to do while standing behind a coffee bar in a green apron with my name stitched on it, prominently displaying the well known logo. I felt like I was part of the corporate Starbucks fabric. In short, I hated it. So I quit...

Two weeks later I booked my first print job, a nationwide billboard campaign for *The Art of Shaving*, and since then I have

4

been able to sustain myself through acting work. I had help, I'm not gonna lie. I sometimes had to borrow money from my girlfriend at the time, and I am lucky to have incredible friends who I can rely on with my life. All in all I've been a working actor in LA for the last 5 years, which puts me in a pretty small group of people. But I still struggle. It's a constant battle between letting the job to job situation and subsequent financial insecurity drive you near mad with anxiety, or surrendering to it all and trusting that something will come along. Why subject myself to this? Beats me. Maybe someday I'll be able to wrap my mind around it. Maybe I'm just afraid of a 'normal' life. Or maybe it's truly a deep calling to express myself through the art of storytelling, and to contribute in that way to the evolution of the human collective. Who knows... Point is, I'm *this* guy. And now you have a bit of an idea of who's talking to you before I drag you along on this journey, which - as you've probably figured out by now - has pretty much everything to do with Bernie Sanders and the political revolution of 2016.

Now, if anyone had told me before May 2015 that I would ever be engaged in a presidential campaign in any way, shape or form I would have called them a fool straight to their face. I was staying as far away from anything politics in my life as I could manage. The mere thought of the meaningless speeches politicians gave all day in between stuffing their own pockets while watching the majority of the country struggle, made my head ache. So no, thank you. No politics for me. Not globally, not nationally, not on the state level or city level or any level else you can think of. Of course I didn't know then that this is exactly how the political, the financial and the media establishment manage to get their way: through us looking the other way. Literally hundreds of millions of us looking the other way, and giving them carte blanche. Well, that was me before 2015. And then things changed one day in the month of May that year...

I was stunned! I had just watched a speech by a completely

unknown democratic presidential candidate - a senator from Vermont - by the name of Bernie Sanders. 'Bernie', I had chuckled. 'That used to be my nickname as a kid.' And then he blew me away: not only was this man speaking with an authenticity I had never before seen in a politician - he addressed *everything* that mattered! 'Am I dreaming?' I thought. This old guy with his messy hair and pressing urgency in his hoarse voice didn't only speak of the crippling effects big money in politics had on basically everything, he also brought up prisons for profit, universal healthcare, paid maternal leave, broken foreign policy, overspending within the military complex, high drug prices, the danger of fracking and the need to move away from fossil fuels, substantially raising the minimum wage, providing a path toward citizenship for undocumented immigrants to bring families together as opposed to tearing them apart, and so on and so on. 'Who is this?' I thought. 'And where did he come from?' I soon learned that Senator Sanders had been well known to politically interested people for decades, and that he had been fighting for justice, equality and democracy basically his entire adult life. Now everybody knows that, of course.

Let me fast forward a bit, since the story of this book isn't really about how awesome Bernie Sanders is - if you're reading this you're probably well aware of that - it's more about how we all dealt with things going South as the primary season came to a shocking and disappointing end, despite an unprecedented effort by millions of Americans to put Bernie Sanders in the office he belonged: the oval one.

One of the last primaries in the Democratic race of 2016 was California on June 7th. My state. And really the last hope for the Sanders campaign to overtake Hillary Clinton in pledged delegates. We worked our butts off. We volunteered, we registered new voters, we donated, we contacted the media, we spoke to everyone we knew. But we never even had a chance... The California election turned into one of the most crushing events of the primaries: in an unprecedented show of bias Hillary

Clinton was declared the presumptive Democratic nominee by the big news networks the day before, resulting in low voter turnout and a general feeling of defeat and hopelessness among all Bernie supporters. This was not democracy: this was a machine pushing their agenda against the will of the people. The unfathomable ways the elections themselves were handled are well documented, and I'll leave it to you to inform yourself about the details online. Try not to cry.

Now it was the day after. I had just watched a video of President Obama's endorsement of Hillary Clinton. And boy, was it a sucker punch: the leader of the United States of America, land of the free, home of the brave, and self avowed bringer of justice, freedom and democracy to the rest of the world, had just called a woman who was under two FBI investigations, was deemed dishonest and untrustworthy by over 60% of the American people, and whose apparent collusion with the Democratic party and the big news networks/newspapers throughout the Democratic primary left millions of voters outraged 'the most qualified candidate for president in the history of the country.' I felt more than let down. I felt betrayed. And completely devastated. 'Is this truly the state of things? Is it this bad? Is there nothing left but lies, corruption and cronyism within the political ruling class?' I thought. 'Are we completely powerless against this machine that seems to have lost even the last wire of connection to the people it's supposed to represent and take care of? God help us.' Tears stung my eyes. I made a halfhearted attempt to hide them from the people entering and exiting the post office on Vermont & Franklin, where I had just picked up my mail. It wasn't really worth the detour on my way to the gym - mostly spam. Worries surfaced in my mind... 'When will I get paid for my most recent job? How much money will be left after my agency and my manger got their cut, and how long will it last? Is there any work coming my way in the near future?' Ahh, the fun existence of an actor in LA: never ending financial uncertainty. I tried to not get overwhelmed by it all, but it was hard not to. 'If it's all just a big circus then why am I trying anyway?' I thought. 'If our President has no problem looking us in the eye and lying to us in the most blatant way, then why are any of us trying? What is the point, if the leaders who are supposed to represent us instead represent only corporate giants and their club of rich and powerful friends? Ugh...'

Eventually some relief set in. Or maybe something in me just resigned to the hopelessness I was feeling. Tears were still hanging on my cheeks, and as I breathed through my grief and sadness I suddenly found some resolve. I looked down at my light blue Bernie T-shirt. Then over at my white 89 Jeep Wrangler that I had ornamented with a large blue Bernie decal - the famous hair and glasses image - and in that moment I realized something: it didn't matter what Obama said. It didn't matter what Elizabeth Warren said (she had endorsed Hillary Clinton the same day, turning into one of the biggest disappointments of this primary), or any other establishment figure who lacked the courage to be real with the people. Who weren't brave enough to tell us the truth. Bernie had told us the truth! And he awoke us with it. And there was no man, woman or institution powerful enough to put us back to sleep with their siren song. It wasn't possible. The truth has lasting power. Lies don't. I knew the truth now. And nothing Obama could say would ever change that. I was #StillSanders, because I was still enlightened by Bernie's message. So I grabbed my phone, placed my Bernie-covered chest in front of my Bernie-covered Jeep and took a selfie, tears and all. I wanted to capture my emotions. To share the picture on one of the big Bernie Facebook pages, the *Bernie Sanders Activists*, where I was an admin and where the Bernie Jeep already had a bit of a celebrity status. I wanted to let people know that despite feeling low, as I knew all of them felt, I wasn't going to give up.

And this is what I posted:

Devastated by Obama's and Elizabeth Warren's betrayal. But no matter how many establishment puppets fall in line: #StillSanders

I was hoping some of the Bernie supporters following the page would be able to relate. Maybe it would contribute to helping one or the other through this roadblock, because God knows we were struggling that day.

I got in my Jeep, and headed to the gym. A workout would do me good. Release the stress, purge the pressure and the feeling of depression. Once there I checked my phone before putting it in the locker, and what I saw made my heart beat faster: the response to my post was yuuuge! More and more comments kept coming in as I scrolled through, and at the end of the day the post had gotten over 3,000 likes and reactions, and the number of comments clocked in around 500. Wow. What I had shared had struck a nerve. People said they felt what I felt, and that my words and the picture gave them some strength to fight through the day. Elated, I walked for the running track. Taller. Lighter. Carried by all those people's feedback, and the feeling of knowing we all empathized. 'This is how humans should be engaging with each other', I thought. Caring. Supportive. Relating.

I started running. The sense of being inspired kept growing inside me. I felt like I had no weight as I was making my rounds. As if I could run on forever. There was purpose in my steps. There was something powerful in what had happened. And I was racking my brain to figure out what to do with it. I wanted to capture this thing. This ability to lend support. To ease peoples' worries. To be encouraging. Maybe even inspiring. I kept thinking about how I could do what I did with that post on a larger scale. I knew the coming weeks leading up to the Democratic Convention in Philadelphia would be monumentally tough for us all. The California primary had been our last hope - the final straw. The Sanders campaign could have turned things around with a landslide victory, but our hopes had been obliterated before we even knew what was happening. Now there would be immense pressure to give up support for Bernie, and for himself to drop out of the race. It was going to be like a monster wave crashing down on us in form of media propaganda, social media attacks, friends and family members telling us to 'grow up' etc. for the next 6 to 7 weeks. All these thoughts rushed through my head as I kept running, light footed, as if carried on some invisible conveyor belt. And that's when it hit me: running. No, *walking*. All the way across the country, destination Philadelphia. Dedicated to Bernie Sanders and his supporters, to provide a sort of moral lifeline to them until the convention came around. Yes! I could hardly contain my excitement. Adrenaline was pulsing through me. It felt like a large dose of pure inspiration had hit me straight in the core. And then I remembered: 'Shit, the pilot!'...

I had booked a half-hour comedy pilot a few weeks prior. It was a great independent project that had two famous actors attached, and realistic potential to be picked up by a large streaming service like Netflix, Amazon or Hulu. And I had the lead part. But it would shoot in July in NYC a couple of weeks before the Convention, rendering my walk dead on arrival. I felt incredibly disappointed. Why on Earth did it have to be this way? Why was there always some scheduling conflict when two or more great opportunities presented themselves? For several days after I felt torn over this conundrum. But in the end I decided to be sensible and stick to the verbal agreement I had given to the producers of the pilot. The idea of walking didn't just go away, however. On the contrary: more and more fantasies played out in my mind every day. Something about it wouldn't let me go. Was it the political statement I wanted to make? Was it the adventure aspect? Was it my yearning to commit myself as fully as I could to the movement Bernie had started, to flip off the establishment, and let them know that not everyone would fall in line and play by their rules? It was probably a combination of all of the above. But it didn't matter - I had to stop myself. It wasn't going to happen, and so I dedicated myself to preparing for the pilot.

A couple of weeks went by, and negotiations between my agent and the producers stalled. I reassured the producers we would make it work, but as fate would have it, a couple of days after our last conversation I got a call out of the blue and was told that they decided to go with somebody else for the part. They said my agent was being difficult, and they were worried it would only cause more trouble down the line. At the end it turned out they weren't willing to put into contract something they had agreed to verbally, and it was probably best for all involved to part ways. Of course I was still disappointed. My ego was hurt. And I mourned the opportunity of being a major player in what could turn out to be a successful show. It could have been my 'big break', who could say? But soon that feeling went away, and was replaced by excitement: my walk was possible after all!

I immediately started researching. How far would I be able to walk in a day? What would the overall distance be? Which state would I drive to in my Bernie Jeep, and which city would be my starting point there (California was out of the question since I now had less than 5 weeks left)? What kind of shoes would I need? What would go in my backpack? Where would I sleep at night? And so on and so on... I wanted this walk to be a metaphor for Bernie's 50-year-long struggle for justice, and for the fact that the movement he started was always going to be a marathon, not a sprint. In my arrogance and naivety - and to make the whole thing more edgy and adventurous - I told no one about my plans. My only preparation was buying a new pair of running shoes and walking them in so they wouldn't cause blisters once I was on the road. And I did a test. Well, a teeny tiny one at least: I wanted to figure out how fast I could walk a distance of 4 miles, considering I would have to keep the pace essentially from sun up till sun down. It turned out I could do it in just over 50 minutes. My pulse was under 110 by the end of it, so nothing to worry about in that department. I gave myself some leeway, and decided then and there that I could walk at 4 miles per hour basically indefinitely. Which meant 50 miles a day shouldn't be a problem... Boy, oh boy. Did I mention arrogance? Did I mention naivety?

I told my therapist of my plans, and she expressed serious concerns about my safety. I still hadn't decided where to start my walk, and one option was to start in New Mexico. Factors like desert heat hadn't even entered my mind at that point, and I'm glad that she made me aware of it. I know now that the early fantasies of my walk were just that: fantasies. There's a not so small chance that I would be dead now had I started my walk in New Mexico at 100+ in the shade, trying to walk an average of 50 miles a day. There are long stretches of nothing in those areas, and running out of water or overheating could be fatal. You don't realize these things until you're actually out there.

So I recalculated: I had to start in a state with cooler temperatures, and cut down my average mileage. 50 a day seemed more and more daunting the longer I thought about it. Then it hit me: 27 days - the magic number! ($27 was the average contribution to Bernie's campaign, and the number became a symbol for Democracy and for a campaign financed by average Americans - *the people* - instead of billionaires and special interests). I'd start closer to Pennsylvania and walk for 27 days. St. Louis, MO, looked like a good starting point. My average would 'only' be in the high 30s - man, was I dreaming. But that's what I decided on, anyway. I was going to drive to St. Louis in my Bernie Jeep, find somewhere to park it for the month, walk to Philadelphia, and after the convention get a one way flight, pick up the car and drive back to LA. Piece of cake.

I was getting more and more excited as I purchased my backpack including hydration pack (it would hold half a gallon of water), several pairs of comfortable sports socks, protein bars and energy gels, a sleeping bag, a head lamp for night walking, etc. But another feeling began to take shape: dread. I think something deep inside me knew that I wasn't approaching this with the necessary care and reason. I had never done anything like this before - not even close. The farthest I'd ever walked in a day was maybe 10 miles, and that's a high estimate. I had always done sports in my life and I wasn't in bad shape, but I had no survival skills of any kind. There were so many unknowns and my preparation was close to zero. Plus, I hadn't told anyone that I was actually going to do this, and that I planned to head out the next day. Well, that was one thing I couldn't skip over. I needed someone to pick up my mail at least once while I was gone, and - more importantly - it just felt wrong to not tell my closest friends what I was about to do - and I am glad I did. When I broke the news to my pals Ian, Mike and Rodrigo I expected nothing but ridicule and that they'd think me foolish. But they surprised me and actually really dug the idea:

(left to right: Rodrigo, myself, Mike and Ian)

My plan of execution, however, got shredded: Mike let me know that it was insane to borderline impossible to walk 35+ miles a day for almost a month without proper training, especially in the summer heat. He really pressed me to lower the average and find a closer starting point (he was the first one who came up with the idea of 27 miles a day for 27 days). But at that point that just seemed way to easy. Ian was excited about the idea of documenting the journey online in real time, which I hadn't even considered. He convinced me to wait two more days to order a small solar charger for my smart phone so I wouldn't run out of battery somewhere in the middle of nowhere. He also ordered an emergency blanket, tons more protein bars and energy gummies, a windbreaker, and some other stuff I hadn't given any thought to, and - in typical Ian fashion - insisted to pay for everything out of his own pocket. Wow. I simply said *thank you*. Rodrigo told me he would set up a Facebook page over the next few days we would call *Bernie for Bernie,* and then we combined our Dropbox storage, so the guys could help me upload videos and pictures from my smart phone. We decided that it was probably best for me to stay in motels overnight, and not bother bringing a tent to sleep out in the open. Safer, and less of a hassle. And it was safer, for sure. Less of a hassle - not exactly. But more of that later.

I felt much better about everything. My dread was gone. I had a team of reliable friends back home that would help me with all things logistics and the documenting of my journey. I did the math on my schedule, considering I had to delay the walk by two days, and I found I could still make it to the convention in time. The event would be running for four days, from July 25th - July 28th. If I left Los Angeles early morning on June 28th, I could reach St. Louis within two days, and leave there the morning of June 30th, which would get me to Philadelphia on July 26th - 27 days - if everything went according to plan. Only, there was no plan. Even with my friends' support this was still a crazy undertaking. I had done a quick road map, noting down my stops all the way from St. Louis to Philly, which looked realistic to me at the time. I guess you have to go into something like this with some ignorance, believing it's possible and trusting that it will work out somehow. That's how I approached it, anyway.

On Monday night, Mike treated me to a comedy show at the Blind Barber in Culver City (where funnily a recurring theme of settlers traveling cross country hundreds of years ago established itself) and afterward he handed me $270 in cash as a goodbye gift to support my trip. I didn't know what to say - good friends are everything.

I set out at 6 am the next day.

Cross Country

I double and triple checked to make sure I had everything I needed (I didn't want the fun of realizing somewhere halfway through Oklahoma that I had left the solar charger in LA.) And though I had no idea what was awaiting me, I felt the sweet excitement of setting out on an adventure. And I hoped and trusted that the old Jeep with its 143,000 miles wouldn't mind a ride to St. Louis. And back, in a months time.

Did I mention it was a convertible Jeep with nothing but a soft top covering the driver and passenger seat...?

The first thunderstorm hit me a couple of hours outside Albuquerque, NM - my planned stop for the night of June 28th. I had enjoyed the ride immensely so far, despite the heat. Or maybe because of it. A convertible Jeep Wrangler gives you an incredible feeling of freedom driving cross country (the second half of California and all of Arizona had me driving topless and still feeling like I was baked in an oven: Needles, CA, won the contest with 114 Fahrenheit in the shade), as long as it's dry...

Now I was in the middle of a flood of rain and frequent lightning, as giant trucks splashed us - me and the Jeep - speeding past (too dark and dangerous for pictures, unfortunately). The fact that I had been driving for 14 hours already, stops included, didn't make the situation easier. I was tired. Really tired. And the intense focus required to keep this old vehicle safely on the road during a thunderstorm at night drained my last bit of energy. But I stayed the course and made it through, and I finally reached Albuquerque to a light drizzle after 860 miles since setting out from LA. I had inquired on Facebook among members of the *Bernie Sander Activists* group to see if any of my fellow Berners could provide a roof for the night (just fyi: I was basically broke and had no idea how to come up with the $3,000+ for the trip, aside from maxing out my credit cards - which, of course, I ended up doing) and while I didn't find anybody in Albuquerque, a generous lady from Tallahassee, FL, contacted me and offered to pay for my hotel room that night (thank you, Alicea!).

I arrived at the *Howard Johnson* in midtown Albuquerque, where a room under my name awaited me. I was incredibly grateful for this generous gesture by a perfect stranger (though Bernie supporters somehow never felt like strangers, even if we had never met), but all I could think about was sleep. I knew I had to leave at 6:30am the next day to have a chance at making it to St. Louis, which would have me spending even more time on the road: the distance was 1032 miles.

I guess I felt invincible. After a hot bath to warm up my wind-beaten body I went to bed and slept like a rock.

I didn't quite make it on time the next day. I left at 6:45am in a grumpy mood, unwilling and unable to understand why the breakfast buffet didn't provide a lid for my cup of coffee. Didn't they understand what happened to a lidless cup of *anything* when placed in the cupholder of a Jeep that's made for driving off road and was 27 years old (hey, there's the number again)? Well, I knew. Because I'd been splashed with all kinds of liquids before. So I speed-sipped my way to the bottom of my near boiling hot cup of coffee, and set out...

While losing 15 minutes that morning didn't seem like a big deal to me then, I would soon discover how a few minutes here and there quickly became hours. Precious hours. Irretrievable hours. And one of the things I learned during this trip - and which will be coming up again later - is that a day does not negotiate its length with you. A neither does a mile.

After the New Mexico wind had beaten me senseless for a couple of hours, I was now driving trough a large chunk of Texas, my first visit to this gigantic state. I liked it. Something about it feels different there. But maybe that's the South in general. It was also in Texas that I made my final decision regarding my starting point. The closer I got to actually setting out on foot, the more I questioned if I could really do 35 or 38 miles a day on average for such a long stretch of time. The familiar feeling of dread found its way back into my gut, and it made me reconsider my options. It became clear to me that I probably needed to be more realistic in this endeavor. I wanted to make it, after all, and not have to give up after a few days because I was too bigheaded.

I searched for a new starting point, and soon Chicago came to mind. I remembered learning about Bernie's time there as a student, and the now legendary pictures and video of his arrest for protesting segregated housing as a 22-year-old in 1963. They had become proof of a life lived for justice and equality. Incredible, to have a man of such integrity and longevity running for president. How lucky we were. And how fitting would it be to start my walk there, and in a sense trace Bernie's life of activism all the way to the Democratic Convention, where he would participate as a presidential candidate. I researched the address of the arrest, and in an old newspaper article found it to be the corner of 73rd and Lowe. You can probably imagine my expression when Google maps displayed the walking distance from there to the Convention Center in Philly as 734 miles - 27 times 27, almost to the dot. I messaged my friends John-Michael and Becca, who were busy preparing a documentary they would shoot in Philly titled 'The Trouble With Normal' that would attempt to cover truthfully the events around the convention, and I was on board as a producer. They couldn't believe the coincidence - let's call it that, for convenience - and the perfect symbolism of my new starting point. Also, John-Michael's family lived in Chicago, and they were more than happy to keep the Bernie Jeep safe while I was gone. Awesome! Things were starting to fall into place.

Oklahoma was next on my route, and man is it beautiful there. I couldn't stop admiring the lush forests and wide open fields, and I actually had to stop my car to film one of the most picturesque sunsets I have seen in my life. But I also saw a lot of poverty there. One small town in particular - I don't recall the name - was a sad sight: crumbling, shut down buildings. Broken roads. Side walks grown over with untrimmed plants. A feeling of emptiness and total lack of opportunity. A couple of older men sitting by the side of the road seemed resigned to a fate of poverty, and little to no hope for a more promising future. Or maybe they didn't even know that such a thing existed. Maybe they'd spent their whole lives here and were now part of the fabric of this place. Maybe anything else - promising or not - would seem so alien to them they wouldn't be able to recognize it... Who can say? I learned one thing very quickly, however - this wasn't going to be the last poor and crumbling town or city I would encounter on this trip. Not by a long shot. Bernie's words about America's poor and underprivileged weren't just words. They described a harsh and widespread reality. An epidemic, really. Because what else can you call the circumstance of 50,000,000 people living in poverty in the wealthiest country that ever existed, with 80% of the population being close to poverty? You tell me, because I don't know.

I let my impressions sit with me as I kept driving, along with the feelings they stirred. Now remember this beautiful sunset I mentioned? Well, that was somewhere in the middle of Oklahoma. And if you take a quick look at the map and trace the distance to my planned destination for the night - namely St. Louis - you'll see that I was going to be in a world of trouble soon. As I said before: a day doesn't negotiate its length with you. But since I was determined to start my walk on June 30th I had to reach St. Louis that night, tackle the remaining 260 miles to Chicago the next morning, and then hopefully start my walk early in the afternoon after dropping off my car.

Sometimes it would be better to let someone else make decisions for me. Someone less stubborn. Less impatient. More prone to reason.

I finally crossed into Missouri. And if I thought I had been exhausted the night before, then I needed to invent a new word for what I was now... I should have gotten off the road at that point, no question. I had been in the car for 16 hours. It was raining again. And it was cold. I had to fight to keep my focus. And I still had 120 miles ahead of me. I wasn't sure what was happening at first when shadows and pockets of fog on the road ahead of me seemed to shapeshift before my eyes. Then, when I was utterly surprised to see a cartoon lion (he looked like Alex from the movie 'Madagascar') on the side of the highway, who turned out to be nothing but a yellow road sign as I got closer, I knew I was hallucinating. This had never happened to me. And I knew it wasn't a good thing that it was happening now. Not behind the wheel of a moving car. But stopping on the shoulder of some pitch black highway somewhere in Missouri at 2am wasn't safe either, and so I decided I didn't really have another option but to keep going until I'd reach the *Motel 6* in St. Louis - my resting place for the night.

I thank the Universe I made it... I was dead tired when I finally got there. Emphasis on *dead*. I went to bed shivering. I couldn't imagine getting up seven hours later to drive another long stretch. And I hadn't even started walking yet. What the Hell was I thinking?

I woke up to gray skies, and though I physically felt about 70, the world was in order again. No cartoon animals or weird shadow beings anywhere. I gave myself a little more time than planned before leaving, and recorded a quick video for my Facebook page. I had already gotten into the habit over the last two days, and tried to document whatever felt important. The country, the people, my impressions, my thoughts, my feelings. Or just to break down logistics. When I saw my face in the camera this morning I knew this clip would be about how exhausted I was: I looked tired and old. 'Am I pushing myself too hard?' I thought.

On my way out of St. Louis I got breakfast at McDonald's. Unfortunately, one of the things that became clear to me early on was the fact that I wasn't going to have the luxury of being choosy with my diet on this journey. Unlike Los Angeles and other coastal cities, most of America doesn't have a large number of culinary options on every street corner. And while I'm sure they exist, my pressing schedule meant I would have to make due with whatever was on the way - which was mostly fast food restaurants and gas stations.

While I slurped down a seriously underwhelming cup of McDonald's coffee in the parking lot, I let the mood of the place sink in. I hadn't seen much of St. Louis driving in late last night (aside from this large, beautiful orange ball that was floating over some high rise buildings. 'How cool', I remember thinking to myself, 'surely the city decided that this was a neat piece of artsy architecture that would catch people's eye coming in off the freeway. Edgy. Unique. I like it. Reminds me of a planet. Like the moon. Just kind of red-ish...' It *was* the moon). Now it was daylight, my hallucinations were gone, and I took in the area. I watched the people around me. It was depressing, to be perfectly honest. I'm sure my fatigue played a part, and the area I was in might not reflect the majority of St. Louis. But there was no way to ignore that people were poor here, and the way they spoke, the way they carried themselves, the dull look in their eyes left an impression of resignation and hopelessness with me - once again. Yay, America.

I set out. The 260 miles to Chicago seemed like a walk in the park compared to what I did the day before. After a while a large gray shape formed on the horizon over rural Missouri (this was real). It looked like smoke from a huge fire at first, but - lucky for whoever would have suffered from the fire and unlucky for me - it was a huge storm cloud instead. Cue the rain... I had thought sun and heat would be my biggest problem on this trip, only so far it seemed more like a British winter than an American summer. But as Austrians will tell you when you complain about getting wet in the rain: 'You're not made of sugar.' And neither was my trusty Jeep. And so we finally reached Chicago, IL. Or I should say Elmhurst, which is about 30 minutes outside the city. That's where John-Michael's family lived - the Damato's - and that's where I would park my Jeep for the next month.

I was welcomed with open arms by John-Michael's parents Wanda and Dave, and his brother Jeremy. Their kindness and generosity were reassuring and comforting after the tiring 2,200 mile drive I had finished in less than two and a half days. And in hindsight it was a preview of how kindly I would be treated by perfect strangers along the way. This country is full of wonderful people. Some don't know this, but it's true:

(Wanda and Jeremy Damato)

The Damato's fed me and expressed great admiration for what I was about to do. It was heartwarming, but I also thought they were purposely exaggerating to make me feel good. In hindsight I believe they weren't. They probably just knew better than I what I was getting into. Wanda and Dave offered their house to rest, and even to stay the night before setting out, but I thankfully refused. With the added drive to Chicago time was already running away from me, and I was dead set on heading out that same day - June 30th.

Before I left I flung my rain tarp on the Jeep to keep it dry over the coming weeks. The Damato's neighbor Tom offered to secure it. 'It'll get windy here', he let me know. 'Nah, it'll stay put', I told him. 'See, I can wedge it in here and here. It'll easily hold.' He laughed, and insisted. Then he went on to strap the thing down like a tornado was about to come through, which I thought was clearly excessive (I have since heard stories from several Chicagoans about the vicious winds there, and I made a mental note that in the future I'll simply keep my mouth shut when I don't know what I'm talking about).

Dave handed me a last minute gift before he hugged me goodbye: it was a bright orange rain poncho. He said it had been sitting in the house for over a decade, but it was still newly wrapped, and maybe it would be of service to me on the road. I thanked him and stored it away in my backpack, thinking I'll probably never use it since I had a windbreaker that was surely rain resistant. Except, it wasn't, but I didn't know that at the time. And so Dave's little gift would turn out to be my savior several times later down the road...

Neighbor Tom was so kind to offer me a ride to my starting point, which was 45 minutes away. He saved me a lot of effort, time and money getting an Uber or taking the train instead. We worked our way through rush hour - it was already 5pm at that point - and eventually the GPS told us we were getting close to our destination: 73rd & Lowe. I should have expected that the neighborhood we were driving into was poor, and almost exclusively African American. 'Of course', I thought. 'This is where Bernie protested segregated housing.' Was it surprising that not much had changed since the 60s, considering the painfully slow progress this country has made and is making in the fight against racism in all its forms? It wasn't. Unfortunately we're not even close to racial justice and equality in the United States of America. Whoever pretends otherwise is not being real.

Tom gave me his number in case anything went wrong and I needed a pick up. Such a good guy. We shook hands, I grabbed my backpack, stepped out onto the street, and watched him drive off. 'This is it', I thought, as I looked around. 'I'm finally here.' I had already started to feel a mix of anxiousness and anticipation during the last minutes in the car. And now I had arrived. This was the spot Bernie Sanders had been arrested at 53 years ago. For being courageous. For being a man of compassion. A man willing to stand up for what he knew was right in his heart, even if most around him didn't agree. Even if it was totally unpopular. Even if it probably made him feel isolated and alone, living in a world where most people couldn't understand what he knew to be true: that we're all the same, no matter what color our skin. That we're all connected. That our planet is mother to us all, and that each and every one of us deserves to be treated equally.

This brave act and the proof we now had in form of pictures and video was one of the main catalysts for how intensively I gave myself to the Bernie Sanders campaign. I mean, I was totally on board two minutes into seeing him speak for the first time over a year before, but when I found out for how long this Senator from Vermont had fought the good fight - that he was a true servant to the people, especially the poor and underprivileged - there was no more holding back. I was all in. At this point I had almost maxed out my campaign contributions, despite my own financial situation. I had volunteered through phonebanking, making over 2,500 calls to potential voters. I spent every free minute on social media, sharing, liking, commenting, organizing, arguing, contributing, and I talked about Bernie with everyone who wanted or didn't want to hear about him. Looking back I probably sacrificed more than I should have - like so many others out there. I'm not Superman, and I can't save the world by myself. But it was hard to draw a line. To know when it stopped being healthy. I know now I should have been more attentive to my fiancee in those days. I regret that now. She deserved better than me sitting next to her with my phone in hand, reading the latest article, or comparing polls, hours on end. And though I know it's not the reason we had separated a couple of months prior to my walk, I knew I could have done better. I think at the end of the day we all simply jumped at the opportunity of having one of the greatest leaders this country had ever seen. And we did so with such vigor and urgency that some of us got in over our heads. But was that avoidable? The urgency wasn't made up, after all. The urgency was there. It was real. We knew we had to turn things around. *Now.* Not in 20 years from now.

Well, here I was. This was my final all out effort. I wanted Bernie Sanders to know that we were with him. And that we would follow him all the way. And as crazy as the idea seemed - I felt good about it. It felt right. I took a photo of myself in this historic place. I needed it for my planned post on my page *Bernie for Bernie* and the *Bernie Sanders Activists* page, with which I would announce my walk. I was curious and excited to see people's response. Would they understand what I was trying to do? Would anyone care? After my last post had blown up I wondered if the feedback would be similar this time around. Maybe I would be sorely disappointed. After all, you can't plan to strike a chord. It happens or it doesn't. I didn't know at this point that people's reactions to my walk would exceed even my wildest expectations...

I made sure everything was in place, then fastened the solar charger to the outside of my backpack, and attached it to my phone. I opened the Google maps app, typed *Wells Fargo Center, Philadelphia,* and chose it as my destination. The app asked me for my starting point, and I clicked: *your location.* And after a few seconds, there it was: a simple, blue dotted line that laid out my entire path. Right from where I stood all the way to the convention center in Philly - almost a quarter of the width of the North American continent - which I had 27 days to reach:

10 d 4 hr (735 mi) · via US-30 E

Google maps made it look so easy. Just follow the blue line, right? And I took my first step...

The Walk

Day 1 - planned destination: Hammond, IN

I took in the neighborhood as I set out. It got more run down and sketchy for the first half hour. I hate to put a label on things, but this was definitely not an area one would call 'safe.' People regarded me curiously, even with suspicion. And I couldn't fault them. I must have been an unusual appearance, the only white guy anywhere in sight, wearing a light blue Bernie Sanders T-shirt, shorts in the same color, running shoes and a stuffed backpack, who was reading directions off his phone like he was lost, trying to find his way out of here.

What I saw reminded me of poor areas in Harlem, NY, where I had lived from 2006-2009. I suddenly remembered that this was the South side of Chicago, at that time one of the most violent and dangerous areas in the country. Young children had been shot recently. Innocent bystanders gunned down in gang related shootings. But the thought quickly left my mind. I've never been afraid of people in my life, and I wasn't going to start now...

I felt good physically. Back in Austria, after I had torn my spleen at age 14, the doctors wouldn't let me do any sports that could cause another tear, not even cycling. So during the summer of 1993 I walked everywhere for 3 months. I got into the habit of walking so fast that I could keep up with my friends who were rolling along on their bicycles. I liked walking. And I didn't mind walking fast - my body was used to it. Or my 14-year-old body was. I should have considered the 23 years difference in my assumptions.

You can figure out pretty quickly how fast you're walking just by paying attention to your movements, and I knew I was easily keeping a 4mph pace during the first stretch. Which was just as I wanted it. I had brought two pairs of shoes: a new pair of Asics I was currently wearing, and my old worn out pair of Reeboks I had tied to my backpack. I knew the new shoes weren't fully walked in yet, and I would quickly get blisters at this pace. So after an hour I switched back to the Reeboks. I planned to keep wearing the pair of Asics a bit longer every day, until they felt totally comfortable.

It had been a beautiful day in Chicago. The sunset lent a romantic feeling to my walk. I knew I wouldn't make it out of urban areas on my first day, and so I didn't have to worry about finding stores and restaurants if I needed food or water. I had set my goal at 20 miles and - having left at 6pm - I thought I should be able to reach my first resting place before midnight, breaks included. It would start me off a bit behind on my average mileage of 27 a day, but I was confident I would be able to make up for it the next day. That was the theory...

Slowly but surely night fell over Chicago on this June 30th of 2016, and I still felt fresh and good. I was a bit ahead of time and filled with confidence. I even remember recording a video, making jokes about abandoning my walk and going gambling instead, as I walked past a casino. I felt free and unencumbered. An inspiring thought crossed my mind: 'What if this is what I was born for? What if this is my destiny? Maybe the promise of being a successful actor in Hollywood was just a way to lure me to the States 10 years prior, but this was the real thing. My name is *Bern-hard* after all! That can't be an accident, can it?' I've gotten so used to smart phone communication I feel compelled to put an emoji here - one with an embarrassed grin. I'm saying that because as I'm writing down these thoughts now they sound ridiculous and ego-inflated. But there's another aspect to this, and it's one that I didn't really understand until later on, when it was all over: these grand thoughts and fantasies about what I was doing and the meaning it possibly had to the world, were necessary. They had a purpose. Because in the coming days and weeks they would get me through moments and sometimes hours of what I would have considered unbearable pain up to that point... So I want to appreciate them. Everything has two sides.

The first long stretch of 4 miles presented itself as I passed the giant BP oil refinery in Whiting, IN (I didn't realize that I had already crossed the state line until later). I couldn't help but think of Bernie's urgent warnings regarding the environment. About our responsibility to separate our energy needs from fossil fuels and gas - if we wanted future generations to have an inhabitable planet to live on, that is. The huge factory blowing thick smoke into the night and the massive oil containers looked so outdated. 'Their time is past', I thought. 'We don't need this anymore. We know now how to harness wind energy and the incredible power of the sun. They're inexhaustible resources from a human perspective. All this has become unnecessary and destructive.' But greed justifies any means to ensure profit for shareholders or a handful of people sitting on some board. Personal responsibility so easily gets lost, especially when corporations grow to such a massive size that individuals are reduced to tiny cogs in a giant wheel.

When I finally came to the end of that straight, though, my pondering these issues had long ceased. And I had learned something new: 4 miles is a long, long, long stretch. It's much easier to walk for half a mile, take a right, then 0.2 miles until the next turn, etc. Little goals help the mind immensely. I'd soon discover more and more the truth behind that.

Not long after - it was now about 10pm - and out of nowhere fatigue covered me like a cloak of lead. My backpack suddenly seemed a lot heavier than it had felt minutes ago. The rush of excitement and the increased adrenalin my body had produced quickly started to wear off. I suddenly realized that I was somewhere I'd never been. That it was late at night in this strange industrial suburb. That I still had over 6 miles to go until I could rest for the night - a distance that seemed more daunting with every passing minute - and that I had barely even scratched the surface of the total mileage that was ahead of me. 'Jesus... Well, I won't get there by standing around', I thought to myself. 'So onward.'

It's fascinating how differently we perceive time depending on our psychological state: the first 4 hours had flown by. I had barely noticed them. Now every minute seemed to pass twice, three times even. My pace slowed noticeably. I was doing somewhere between 3-3.5pmh. The 4mph I had believed I could do indefinitely were now out of the question. Ian connected with me through Zello (a phone app that works a bit like a walky talky). He wanted to know if I was okay, since the live GPS signal my phone was supposed to send out wasn't showing on his end. I realized I hadn't opened the live tracker app before heading out. I corrected that, and reassured him I was doing fine. It was good to hear a familiar voice in this strange and abandoned concrete environment. 'I'm definitely feeling it', I told Ian. 'But I think I can still make it before midnight.'

I soon found out I couldn't. I had to take more and longer breaks, and I was simply exhausted. The last 2 miles, especially, seemed monumental, and the clock had long struck midnight before I finally felt the relief of spotting the blue-lit *Motel 6* sign about 0.3 miles ahead. But even then I thought I wouldn't make it: my right foot had started to hurt a few minutes prior. A sharp pain on the inside of my arch, halfway between toes and heel. I was almost limping now. I tried to be as careful as possible. The thought of injuring myself, and possibly endangering the rest of the journey frightened me to the core (now I know the damage was already done at that point).

Walking this slowly I felt like I wasn't making any progress at all. It wasn't unlike a dream where you're running but strangely not moving forward. 'How can the motel be in such close reach and yet so damn far away?' I thought. I gave up protesting and decided to trust that the laws of physics still applied, and then -

finally - I saw myself walking through the office door. The florescent light was harsh and unfriendly, but I couldn't think of a better place to be anywhere in the world. Actually, I could - a room with a bed. After all I still had to walk there. I must have been a sorry sight to the lady behind the counter. Pale. Sweaty. Bending over from fatigue and exhaustion. I couldn't wait to sleep.

I managed to stay awake long enough to take a hot bath. It soothed my muscles, but the feeling of being utterly depleted didn't go anywhere. I got cold shivers as I crawled under the sheets... 'That's not good, I'm on the verge of getting sick', I realized. I had scheduled to set out much earlier the next day. Latest by 10am. And I already got the feeling that wasn't going to happen.

After waking up and feeling awful, I decided to sleep an hour or two longer than planned. I couldn't set out like this and repeat what I had done the day before. Wait, not repeat: *add* another 7 miles, if not 10. I felt overwhelmed. It seemed impossible all of a sudden. I had finished only one day so far, and not even hit my average mileage. What was I going to do...?

I got up for one. I knew right away that things weren't good physically. Not that my muscles were too sore - that wasn't the problem. I was simply spent. There was no strength in my body. Plus, I now felt a prominent pain in my right knee, and it was slightly swollen. My foot hadn't stopped hurting either. The pain wasn't as acute as it had been on the last stretch the prior night, but it was not something I could ignore, that much was clear. I had hurt myself in some way. I could only hope that it wasn't too serious, and that I would feel better soon...

I hadn't decided on my next destination yet. The route I had worked out before leaving Los Angeles had St. Louis, MO, as a starting point, not Chicago. So it was of no use to me anymore. I would simply have to decide my resting points as I went along, and thankfully I had the guys back home to help me so I could focus on things like keeping hydrated, taking videos or pictures, and: walking. Because - as I quickly realized - letting my thoughts wander or taking in nature as my legs did their own thing, wasn't going to happen...

Day 2 - planned destination: Someplace, IN

Shortly before noon I set out. The pain was manageable, but it was an almost constant negotiation of where to put my weight - heel, toes, outside or inside of my foot - and at times I purposely limped to give my right foot and knee a break. I learned quickly that the body doesn't react well to these kinds of tactics. You do that for a long enough time you start straining some other joint, muscle or tendon, and then you have to relieve *that* area, and so it goes back and forth until no part is left unharmed. To make matters worse, Ian informed me that I only had two choices as far as stops for the coming night were concerned: I could end my day in Valparaiso, IN, which was 24 miles from my last stop, or add another 15 miles to reach the next one. So I either had to make a tough call and take another cut to my average mileage, or... 39 miles. Gulp. I held on to my hope that it was somehow possible, though not for long. Before the first hours had gone by I decided that Valparaiso would be as far as I could make it, and I would have to catch up on miles in the days following.

Presently, I discovered that I had crossed the first state line sooner than expected. I didn't know that Chicago is all the way in East Illinois and so I was surprised to find out that I had been in Indiana since the night before.

Indiana... I had never been to this state. The only thing that came to mind was a city called Lafayette. The reason being, that - having been obsessed with Guns n' Roses as a teenager - I could still remember that W. Axl Rose was born and raised in Lafayette,

35

IN. And somehow, after 7 years in Los Angeles, where he and I now both resided, I still hadn't run into him to tell him that he was a little Austrian boy's hero (add to bucket list). Anyway, Lafayette wasn't going to be on my route, unfortunately, so any silly ideas of finding Axl Rose's childhood home and taking a selfie in front of it quickly evaporated. Instead I got to see a different place: Gary, IN. I would learn a few days later from a Bernie delegate named Michael Gibino - a marathon athlete who ran all the way from Minnesota to Philadelphia, and who I was in contact with due to the similarity of our journeys - that he was told to avoid Gary. Had I known, that despite being a small town, Gary had a reputation beyond Indiana for being a dangerous place, maybe I wouldn't have filmed people and surroundings there as blatantly as I did. I still would have walked through it, though, because I sure as Hell wasn't going to add even more miles to my walk, unless absolutely necessary. Also, something in me refuses the concept of avoiding an area because it's 'dangerous.' If it is, it's because people there are in need. If they weren't they wouldn't be stealing, or killing each other over drugs. And isolating them and giving them a wide birth isn't going to solve the problems of that community. But if you've never seen Gary, IN, let me tell you - it's a shocking sight. Something like a mini version of Detroit, MI (the pictures don't really do it justice):

Abandoned, ramshackle buildings. Bars and restaurants with boarded windows, long shut down for business. Old furniture and trash on the overgrown sidewalks. An oppressive atmosphere hanging like a dark cloud over the town. Suspicion in people's looks. No hope. No opportunity. Junkies staring out on the street through empty eyes. It was sad. Really, really sad. 'This is how people have to exist?' I thought. 'What else is going to come from this but crime, drugs and violence?' The heavy impression the place left on me pushed aside my own pain and discomfort for a while. I took a rest under a tree, taped up a couple of blisters that tried to sneak their way in without me noticing, ate and drank, and assessed my situation. My right foot was still hurting, and the hope of this going away was fading fast. I would likely make it worse by continuing on, but what choice did I have?

Before I went on I remembered that I still needed to make the post about my walk on Facebook. I had wanted to wait a day or two, to not embarrass myself by making a big announcement and then having to give up for some reason. And even though I wasn't feeling great I decided to upload my picture and let everyone know what I was doing:

I'M MARCHING FROM CHICAGO *to* PHILLY
27 MILES A DAY FOR 27 DAYS - IN TIME FOR THE DNC, IF ALL GOES WELL.

'I started out where Bernie was arrested in 1963 for protesting segregation.'

BERNHARD FORCHER
ACTOR - DIRECTOR - ACTIVIST

WE ARE THE MEDIA & FOR BERNIE SANDERS

I will upload clips, and you can follow my path via live GPS.

FB.COM/WEARETHEMEDIA2016

(This version was created and posted by *We Are The Media* soon after they picked up on my original post. Thank you, Andrew!)

After marching through a charming little place called Hobart, IN, the surroundings began to change. This was more like the kind of landscape I was expecting to come through on the majority of my walk: rural. Fields, meadows and forests to both sides of the highway. A gas station or a farm every few miles. And other than that just me, traffic and wildlife. Speaking of wildlife: one of the lasting memories of this experience will unfortunately be the ungodly amount of roadkill I walked past. I estimate the overall number of dead animals - large ones like raccoons, beavers, deer, foxes, possums, squirrels, etc - at somewhere between 1,500 and

2,000. I saw another one every few minutes. Some completely flattened, leveled on the concrete, some without visible injuries, who were probably hit in the head, others decomposed or taken apart by scavengers. Some with their mouths open like in a horrible death scream, some more peaceful, for lack of a better word. But it was heartbreaking every time. That day, when I saw a raccoon family of four - two large ones and two babies - all squashed next to each other, I couldn't help but cry. I've watched raccoons in my backyard at night, and the way they communicate and take care of each other is beautiful. They're highly social beings, with a wide range of emotions and their own individual experience of the world. Just because their brains don't have a human's capacity doesn't make them any less precious. But if I liked it or not, this sight would become a constant on my journey, that much I knew after day one...

Presently, day two had a different kind of challenge in store for me: about halfway through my 24 miles I hit an 11-mile straight. I took a deep breath. 'At least by the end of it I'll be less than a mile away from the *Super 8* motel Ian reserved for me', I thought. 'One step at a time.'

It was a warm day. Not too hot, thankfully. But now that I was breaking into the second half of today's distance, my body started to revolt. I had completely exhausted myself the night before, and - though a good night's sleep gave me a cushion for today - now I was starting to pay for it. And a lot earlier than I would have liked. One thing, however, kept my spirits up for a while, and that was the completely overwhelming response to my post: at the end of the day it had over 6,300 likes and reactions, and more than 1,000 comments! I had hoped Bernie supporters out there would understand what I was doing. That maybe they would appreciate the symbolism of this gesture, but I had not expected this level of support and encouragement. It was an incredible feeling. Unfortunately, I needed to force myself to stop reading the comments, since every time I checked the phone I simultaneously saw how little progress I was making, and that would only be a mental hindrance. Like checking your watch every five minutes on a long flight - I'm sure you've done it. Time begins to stand still when you do that. Like it knows, and it's teasing you.

Meanwhile my right foot, shin and knee continuously got worse. 'I need to find a way to deal with the pain', I thought to myself. I knew there was a place I could go to in my mind - a sort of meditation, if you will - where I could become more of an observer to my body, than be completely identified with it. I believe that's how people who train themselves in techniques like these for many years can endure unimaginable pain. Like Buddhist monk Thích Quang Duc, who burned himself alive in Saigon in 1963 without moving a muscle or uttering a sound - all to protest the persecution of Buddhists by the South Vietnamese government. I'm not great at this, by any means, but thank God this wasn't like being burned alive...

I focused intensely on being fully present, and as if I was remote controlling my body, instead of *being* it. I kept any unwanted thoughts at bay and my eyes low, trained on the ground before me. I didn't want to give my mind a chance to fall into despair at the never-ending straight ahead and to tell me to stop. And this tactic did work - for a while. After about an hour I took a break. I sipped on my Gatorade bottle, chewed on some energy gummies, and rested for a few minutes. I looked for some shade, and did some stretching. I hoped I had put about 4 miles behind me as I hesitantly checked my phone. Nope - 2.7. God, this was going to be endless! As much as my 'meditative walk' had helped me get through the last stretch, the focus it required mentally exhausted me more than I could afford, and so I resigned to the thoughts flooding back into my mind and the feeling of disappointment that made itself known in my gut. And with it the pain returned: I *was* my body again.

As I continued things slowly but surely got worse. The shin muscles on my right leg began burning. It was intense, especially when I pushed off. Combined with my sensitive knee and the sharp pain in my foot, putting my full weight on my right leg was now out of the question. I fell into a slight limp - I'd say 70% on my left, 30% on my right - just trying to set one foot in front of the other. That's how another endless hour went by.

The sun was setting when I let myself slide down the wall outside a gas station, at which I had just stocked up on supplies. I was wiped. And sitting down made me realize how little my body had left to give. I felt a surprising chill as the first shade covered me, and I couldn't help but thinking that things - considering I was soon going to walk in the dark - were about to get much, much harder.

My backpack seemed to be filled with chunks of ore as I got back on my feet. It was hard to believe how vulnerable I felt. A few days earlier I had been at the gym, running a 5k with a powerful stride and with ease. Now I felt like my aching muscles and bones belonged to the body of a fragile old man. 'Come on', I told myself. 'Doesn't matter if you're slow. Just keep going, at some point you'll get there.'

My limp got worse with every step. I was now moving at 2mph, maybe even slower. I had to stop once again to put on my windbreaker. The night had cooled the air noticeably, and the sweat on my skin began to feel uncomfortable. Every interruption made the task harder. Every distraction reminded me of the dreadful state I was in. I never cry from despair... I cry seeing others suffer, or because of heartbreak or extreme joy. I cry in the movies, when a story pulls me in on a deep emotional level. But never because of despair. It's just not how I respond to that feeling. Now I did. I'll tell you without shame that I whimpered like a lost child. The night seemed threatening and cruel. It enhanced everything I felt, and made it worse. I was consumed with hopelessness and fear. All my defenses had crumbled. The situation seemed so utterly dire - especially with the looming 700 miles still ahead of me - that I just couldn't see a way. Then it all became a blur, and after what seemed like eons in purgatory I reached the end of that 11-mile straight. 'One mile left. God, help me get there', I prayed.

I passed the outskirts of Valparaiso. It's hard to express how good it felt to see lights and people. But my limp was so bad now and my pace so slow, I didn't seem to be moving at all. 'How can it still be 0.8 miles?!' I thought, incredulous. Minutes felt like hours, and space seemed to expand looking ahead. A group of young guys walked past me, out on the town. I know it sounds funny, but the ease they moved with astounded me. One of them stopped. He asked if I was okay. I told him I had been walking all day, and that my legs hurt. But I was almost at my destination. 'Thanks for asking.' They waved goodbye, and moved on.

I had 0.4 miles left when I saw a fast food restaurant on the side of the road. It was 10:30pm, and it was still open. I couldn't imagine anything more beautiful than a bed, but I knew I needed some food before going to sleep... If what I already described didn't do the job of relating my overall state, I want you to consider my thoughts as I assessed the situation: the restaurant was on *my* side of the road. I didn't have to cross the street to get there. It was about 60, maybe 80 feet from where I stood. There was a slight incline, maybe a 3-foot increase in elevation to reach the entrance. I really, *really* negotiated this with myself before I decided in favor of food...

I somehow made it through the door, limped for the counter and ordered a chicken sandwich with fries, and a lemonade. The young ladies who worked there were incredibly sweet. I told them about my walk, and - since they loved Bernie - they also loved what I was doing. Seeing I was in pain, one of them reached into her bag and handed me a bottle of Ibuprofen. It was nearly full. 'Keep it', she said. I had no energy to refuse, so I simply thanked her and dragged myself to a table. Sitting down felt so good, but knowing I still had half a mile to go to my motel left me restless. I basically inhaled the food. In that moment I couldn't care less about breaking with my vegetarian diet. I just needed carbohydrates, protein and sugar. Before I left, one of the employees - her name was Vega - agreed to tell me on camera why she liked Bernie Sanders. Young people just got it. They knew their future was at stake, on so many levels. And they knew the clock was ticking. We could see it reflected in the unprecedented support for Bernie by young voters in virtually every state. How many times have I heard millenials being described as 'lazy.' A thankless generation that got everything handed to them and just didn't care - so wrong. They cared very much. But they were also dealt a difficult hand. Born into a society so overloaded with information through the explosion of the internet and social media, and having the bad luck of being the generation that was going to really pay for the terrible mistakes of the past. It's not easy to remain optimistic and hopeful under these circumstances.

I said goodbye, and headed out to tackle the final stretch. Somehow resting and getting some food in me had done nothing to make walking more bearable. I fell right back into the same dark place. 10 steps or 10 miles - anything seemed too far at this moment. But I pushed forward. 'Soon it's going to be over, come on', I whispered to myself, in between moans of ache and complete exhaustion. When I finally saw the yellow-red *Super 8* sign, I could hardly believe that this day was actually about to come to an end. I fixed my eyes to that 8 as I crossed a wide road. The simple task of lifting my legs onto a curb felt monumental. Stepping off one was just as bad. I sought out the grass on the side of the road. It hurt less to walk on grass.

Soon I found myself heading for the entrance of the Motel. I had made it. I had *actually* made it. I was so happy to see the two young guys behind the counter. I joked that they better have a room or I would have a mental breakdown, ha ha. 'Sorry, we're booked out for the night', they told me. 'Wait, what? No, no, no', I uttered. 'My friend reserved a room. Please check again.' Nope. They were booked out, and none of the rooms were under my name. I wasn't sure if to laugh or cry. I called Ian, who was as furious as I've ever heard him. He knew the shape I was in, and he was worried about me. He tried to get the staff to fix their mistake, but to no avail. We agreed then and there that I would henceforth boycott *Super 8* on this trip, but that didn't fix my problem: it was nearly midnight, I was running on my very last reserves and I now had to find a different place for the night. The Yelp app on my phone told me that there was a relatively cheap option a mile away, which was absolutely out of the question. And so I decided to bite the bullet and head for the *Country Inn Hotel*, where a room would cost me $140 for the night. The worst part was that I had to walk half a mile *back* in the direction I came from... You can probably appreciate how utterly obscene that notion appeared to me at that point. I called ahead to make sure they weren't booked out as well (they weren't) and after about a half hour I was finally watching my hand inserting a lovely plastic key card into a door marked 21: my luxurious room for the night. I entered, thanking whoever was watching over me, dropped my stuff in a corner and immediately let in a hot bath.

I inspected my leg: a large red circle had formed on my shin, and it didn't stem from the skin. It came from the muscle underneath:

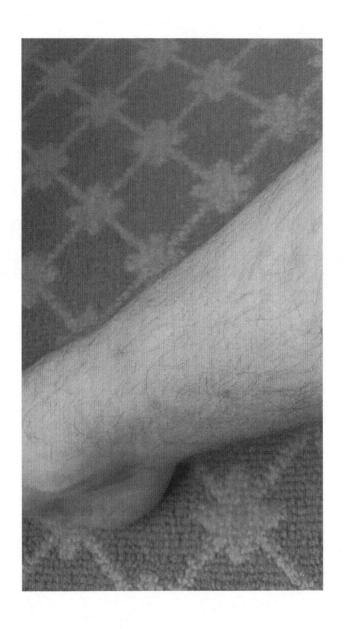

There was another discoloration on the inside of my foot, right on the arch, where the sharp pain came from:

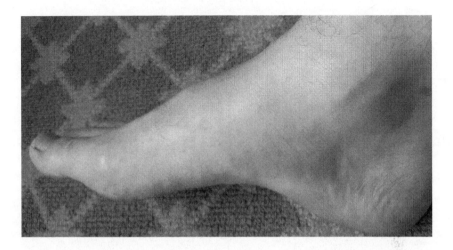

Before I went to bed, I soaked in the hot water I had filled with epsom salts, hoping it would soothe my muscles enough so I could keep going the next day. Afterwards I slipped under the soft sheets, incredibly appreciative of the comfort they provided, and sent out a quick prayer to the Universe, asking for fast recovery. And then, like on any night during this journey, I fell asleep immediately.

Day 3 - planned destination: ???

The next morning I could hardly walk to the bathroom. I was injured, there was no doubt. I talked to my friends back in LA, and Rachel - one of Ian's work colleagues who became a great addition to my support team - told me her mother, a nurse, had looked at the pictures of my foot and shin I had sent. And by the looks of it and from the way I had described my pain, it was almost certainly both shin splints and a stress fracture. Now, I've done a lot of sports in my life: I was in a soccer team as a kid, played competitive tennis for several years, took part in decathlon tournaments as a teenager, and then fought my way through ballet and jazz dance classes during my musical theater education in my early twenties (which is sport, make no mistake). I broke four toes during three years of ballet, but I was lucky to never actually injure my legs or feet in a serious way during all those years - all this to say I didn't know what this diagnosis meant.

I decided to do some research myself and sure enough, the causes and symptoms of both the shin splints and the stress fracture couldn't have been describing my situation more accurately: shin splints are micro tears in the muscle and bone tissue caused by overuse along the shin bone. And - surprise, surprise - they occur, among other reasons, through walking or running excessive distances, especially on hard surface. They can be excruciatingly painful (check) and usually diminish and go away completely when the activity is ceased (you mean unlike walking another 690 miles over the next three weeks?). Same thing with the stress fracture: the pain in my foot came precisely from what's called the *metatarsal bones*. Metatarsal stress fractures are also called 'march fractures' because they are often seen in soldiers who march for a long time. While I didn't have a doctor present to confirm the diagnosis, I think you'll agree on the high likelihood that it was accurate. And even if it wasn't: whatever I had and whatever it was called - I couldn't walk. The shin splints were so acute and painful, I couldn't even move my toes without contorting my face.

I called Ian, who told me in his dry British tone: 'I'm sorry, mate. I think you're done.' Ugh. I didn't like his matter-of-factness in that moment. I didn't want a sensible voice. I didn't want someone realistic telling me how things actually were. I wanted someone who would help me keep the dream alive! But I soon conceded. He was right. Later I would find out that even the walk to the breakfast room - approximately 80 feet with no ticking clock whatsoever - was a challenge. The mere thought of the distance I would have to put behind me in the coming days - especially since I was already behind on my average - was laughable. I was so incredibly disappointed...

Zeke, another of Ian's colleagues, who had joined the LA mission control team, suggested to head back to Chicago after I was rested, and to drive the rest of the way in my Bernie Jeep. I could stop in cities along the way and connect with Bernie supporters, take pictures with the Jeep and post them on the page, etc. It was a good idea, but I just couldn't let go of my walk. Rodrigo suggested to get a bike somewhere and cycle the rest of the way, or at least until my foot felt better. Now, that was more like it. But two things got in the way of that: I wouldn't be able to call this whole thing a *walk* anymore. I would be *Biking for Bernie* and in that moment I couldn't think of anything less inspiring. And second - and more importantly - there was a physical issue: when you ride a bike you have to both flex your foot (on the down movement), and extend it (on the up movement). Either of those actions made me cringe at the mere thought - my shin splints wouldn't allow any of that. I could, however, put weight on my foot as long as I didn't move it around. Then there was no pain whatsoever. So when Ian mentioned a scooter I immediately lit up with hope. I had rode a scooter before, and - if I remembered correctly - I would be able to rest my right foot on the board, while pushing off with the left. At least I decided in that very moment that this would be the case. It had to be!

My depressed mood and disappointment evaporated. Maybe it was possible after all? I disregarded the voice of reason ringing out somewhere in my head, telling me that if I went to see a doctor, they would probably tell me to rest, put my leg up for a few days, and then not exercise for at least a month to heal the stress fracture and avoid risking a real fracture, which would mean a cast and crutches for weeks (lalalala...not listening).

Ian told me there was a bicycle store about 0.2 miles from the hotel. I called there and the man on the other end instantly became my best friend when he confirmed that they had a few scooters in the store. But they would close at 3pm since it was Saturday, and with the long 4th of July weekend coming up, this would be my only chance to get a scooter until Tuesday the coming week: I had about an hour.

The friendly guy at the front desk of the *Country Inn* - his name was Vinny - told me he knew someone who drove for Uber, and that he sometimes called him directly through his cell if a guest needed a ride. So that's what he did.

After I apologized in advance for the super short ride, my talkative but very pleasant driver steered his car around exactly two street corners, parked the car and agreed to wait for me outside the bicycle store. I limped inside, hanging on to my hopes that all this would work out somehow. I approached a young salesman and asked about the scooters. He showed me what they had for sale, and after I told him I needed to ride it around the floor for a bit to decide if I was going to buy it, he gave one to me. I put my hands on it. 'Wow, this is definitely built for kids', I thought. The height of the handles was too low for me and it wasn't adjustable. I would have to lean forward to grip them. But I didn't care about comfort. All that mattered to me was that I could move ahead on this thing while healing my injuries. I placed my right foot on it, and grabbed the handles: this was the moment of truth... I gently pushed off with my left foot, slowly steering the scooter down the narrow aisle. My full weight was now resting on my right foot (and partly on my wrists) and it was painless! I felt a huge sense of relief and excitement in my chest as I turned a corner, accelerating as much as the space allowed. Speed didn't matter, I realized. I could go as fast as I wanted, as long as my foot was safe in place. Ha! I could probably catch up on mileage with this thing, until I was able to walk again. It wasn't perfect, and I would have much rather walked every step. But this was an adventure, after all, and improvisation was unavoidable. People would understand, I reassured myself.

I tend to not take in all of the circumstances, set aside time and plan ahead - you've probably figured that out by now. So, safe to say, there would be obstacles coming my way that I had no mind considering in that moment. Such as roads that were not exactly smooth and comfortable to ride on, with a kid scooter that had wheels made of hard rubber and absolutely zero shock absorption. Or the fact that using the same foot to push off all day long would probably cause more trouble...

I needed a path forward and I needed it now, so I allowed myself to believe it would all be smooth sailing from there. I swallowed at the price of the scooter: $220. This journey was quickly becoming my financial ruin. 'I'll have to put it on my credit card', I thought. Money doesn't really count there anyway, right? You carefully squint at your statement once a month, just long enough to see what the minimum payment is, then you quickly make that payment and push the knowledge of your debt deep down to some unconscious place until next month comes around. Ah, capitalism. Beautiful, for those who get to collect the interest. But in that moment I had no mind for my personal debt, or the mine field that our financial system presents to most people in the country: I had a path forward, and was thus in good spirits!

My driver wished me good luck for the rest of my journey as he dropped me off back at the hotel. I showed Vinny the scooter. He chuckled as I told him I was going to keep heading for Philadelphia with it, at least until my limp was gone. That morning before breakfast - and after realizing I needed at least a day to ice my leg and reduce the inflammation - I had come to

Vinny (a Hillary supporter and avid CNN watcher of all things) to tell him I was going to stay another night at the hotel. He had inquired about my Bernie T-shirt, since he was very interested in politics, and - after hearing what my journey was about - had given me a discount of 50% on my second night. Because he appreciated my activism. Even if it was for Bernie Sanders, who was not the candidate he supported. Pretty awesome, right? (Thank you, Vinny!)

The rest of my day consisted of several careful walks to the ice machine and back, putting up my leg, lots of ibuprofen, Mediterranean food and TV. Some show about the mind-boggling state of the American prison industry, and life inside the Hell of it. I can't express in words the disgust I feel toward the injustice of prisons for profit in America. It is modern day slavery, and the United States should be ashamed to its core until the day this tragedy is remedied. But I digress...

I packed my things the next morning with mixed feelings in my stomach: I was looking forward to keeping going, excited and optimistic. And yet, I felt incredibly vulnerable with my injuries and my limp. Again I was setting out without having done any tests or preparation. And riding on the scooter would be very different than walking. I hadn't even considered the problems I could run into with traffic regulations, and the consequences of possibly violating them - namely, the police. After all, I was now on a wheeled vehicle. And from what I could tell looking at the map, there wouldn't be a lot of back road traveling going forward. I was going to have to take busy highways if I wanted any chance at completing this thing in time.

I don't know to this day if it is legal to ride a scooter on a road in traffic or on the shoulder of a highway in the states I went through. My gut told me it wasn't, and I decided it was better to not find out so I could claim ignorance in case I got stopped. Not a very grown up approach, I know. But, hey.

Day 4 - planned destination: Hamlet, IN

Off I went, scooting along the side of the road. My right foot was still and unmoving, and my left one was doing all the work. It felt good to be moving quicker, though I knew I had to be careful. If I started out too fast again it could be the end of my journey, and I wasn't going to let that happen. But that also meant I wouldn't catch up on mileage again, which was especially troubling since I had just lost a whole day to resting my leg.

The next city, Plymouth, IN, was 44 miles away - a distance I couldn't risk - and the only other motel in between me and there was the *Stay4LessMotel*, which looked to be next to the Highway in the middle of nowhere near a tiny town called Hamlet. The *Stay4LessMotel* looked quaint to be polite, but I didn't care where I would stay as long as there was a bed and a bathtub. All I wanted was to heal my foot. And I was confident I could make the 25 miles.

After putting Valparaiso behind me it didn't take long to find out what my challenges for the foreseeable future would be...

One, the roads: every tear in the concrete, every pothole, every bump, every piece of gravel was a direct hit to my wrists and my right ankle - when I was lucky enough to be on otherwise smooth asphalt, that is. Because it would soon turn out that there were long stretches where the road was paved with such a rough cement mix - like gravel glued together - that scooting along it wasn't only going to hurt me more, but it was almost impossible to move forward, period. The wheels on a scooter are really small, and the constant resistance and friction stopped any momentum.

And two, the one-sided movement: about halfway through the day I started to feel the consequences of pushing off with one foot only. A tenderness made itself known in about the same area that I had injured on the right: the metatarsal bones. I knew I had to be very, very careful in this new undertaking. If I injured my left foot as well, it was over. And my legs weren't the only problem now: with the handles being so low I had to constantly lean forward or bend over. You can imagine what that does to your back after ten hours, especially if the movement is exclusively one-sided. The left side of my lower back was tensing up more and more. Sometimes, when the road would go downhill and I didn't have to push to move forward, I was able to fully straighten my back for a few seconds. It meant that I had to steer with the very tippity-tips of my fingertips, but it was possible. It felt like heaven.

Overall this new way of traveling was beyond challenging and it's hard to explain my state that day. I felt vulnerable, and incredibly fragile. Sometimes I was forced to walk, because the road was too rough. It scared the Hell out of me. I knew I needed to let my right foot heal. I just couldn't risk to worsen the shin splints or the fracture. So I used the scooter as a crutch, trying to relieve my foot as much as humanly possible. The whole thing was a tightrope walk: when all you want, really *all* you want, is a surface smooth enough to scoot on so you can heal your injured foot while putting an ungodly amount of miles behind you (which is already a really uncomfortable all-day work out) and - the deafening noise and the danger of being hit by a truck on the shoulder of a busy highway aside - what you get is not only shoulders covered in gravel, but on top of that rumble strips literally every ten feet, you do start to lose your mind after a while. I did, anyway.

All things, good or bad, come to an end. Eventually - after my building frustration had led to angry outbursts at shorter and shorter intervals - I spied the *Stay4LessMotel* sign on the left side of the 30 Highway not too far ahead. I had made it through my first day on the scooter. What a relief. And from what I could tell I hadn't made things worse. In my right foot, that was... I had given my left foot a rough deal, and it made sure to let me know. But at least it didn't feel like another stress fracture. I could still walk on it, if slowly. I was almost more worried about my wrists in that moment, because they were shot. I have quite skinny wrists to begin with, and - with the added weight on my back - trying to relieve my foot by leaning forward and resting more weight on my hands, wasn't exactly safe. The never-ending blows from the rough roads had left their mark. Another thing to be careful about. I felt like I was quickly turning into a man made of glass: couldn't be too fast, couldn't be too rough, couldn't be too much, or I would break. I couldn't even remember what it was like to feel strong and invincible, a state I had enjoyed only four days earlier setting out from Chicago. Then I decided to give myself a break. After all, I had made it. I had put the hard part of the day behind me, and now it was on to the fun: sleep.

I was put off as I saw my room, even considering my fatigue. I knew for $35 I wasn't going to get what I had had the night before, but the shower looked disgusting. The ground and the walls were rust-red, and the water in the toilet looked liked someone had just peed in it and forgotten to flush:

After I spoke to the owners - a really sweet couple, who seemed genuinely concerned after I had arrived later than I said I would - I knew it had nothing to do with cleanliness: the quality of the water in the area wasn't great, and the iron that gave it the yellow color left the shower looking rusty and dirty. They apologized for it and gave me a gallon of bottled water so I didn't have to drink from the pipe. Some of the other guests - most of them construction workers, judging by the equipment on their old pick up trucks - stayed at the motel monthly. They worked in the area, but weren't from here. One had even been there for a year and a half. The owner told me he and his wife wanted nothing more than to get away from Hamlet, IN. I don't know what exactly kept them tied to the place, and I couldn't fault them. Like me they had lived in big cities before, and - though I never saw the actual town of Hamlet - considering this was the only motel in the area, it was probably not exactly a dream destination.

I had to make due without a bath that night, since the room had no tub. But then, even though I knew now it wasn't dirt that made the bathroom look uninviting, I probably would have passed anyway. A shower would be fine.

Day 5 - planned destination: (hopefully) Warsaw, IN

The next morning I slipped into my dirty Bernie T-shirt and set out, leaving the *Stay4LessMotel* behind.

Just as an aside: I brought only my one T-shirt. Reason being, that if I had wanted to wear a clean T-shirt every day, I would have had to bring at least five. It's not like there's a washing machine at every cheap motel in the US, and I would sometimes not get to wash my clothes for a week. And, considering the limited space in my backpack, the maximum amount of T-shirts I could fit would have been maybe three, meaning I would be wearing a dirty T-shirt at some point. So why not save space, bring just one and embrace being gross? So my T-shirt was dirty, who cares? I was alone, after all. And smelling bad was the least of my problems...

I hoped that the roads would be less brutal going forward so my foot would get a chance to heal, but they sucked just as much as the day before. And I soon realized that - while my right foot hadn't gotten worse, and I felt like it would probably get better over time - I wouldn't get away with doing the same one-sided routine I had done the day before. The constant impact of pushing off the concrete was starting to wear my left foot down fast, and I felt the first warning signs I had ignored in my right foot a few days prior. It's really simple: your body sends signals to warn you. Mild pain at first, and if you don't listen, the pain increases in intensity. At some point the warnings are used up and real damage occurs. I couldn't let that happen. I was truly worried. How much could my body take? How would I find the right balance? I knew I had to give my left foot some rest, and whenever the road allowed me to roll downhill a bit, I put both feet on the board, and leaned on my wrists as much as possible. But Indiana isn't exactly an uphill-downhill kind of state (Pennsylvania was going to provide plenty of that fun later on). The country here was flat and I couldn't move the scooter forward without pushing off. Damn!

Things get curiously basic in situations like these: I couldn't walk for more than a few dozen feet here and there, and even that only while leaning heavily on the scooter (I had, however, figured out that I could hang my backpack on the handles, which meant less weight for me to carry). And to ride the scooter I needed momentum. *I* had to be the engine moving it forward, and I only had two feet to do that with. One was injured, and the other was about to be. You can see the limited options at my disposal. But I had to come up with something, and so I decided to risk a very careful attempt at pushing off with my right foot for a change. 'Yeah, no. F*** no! Ouch. Don't make it worse dude!' I scolded myself. You have to first flex your foot and then extend it, doing that. Just like on a bicycle. But what else could I do? I had to find a way to relieve my left foot. I leaned forward, pressing my left knee into the relative softness of my backpack which was now hanging off the handles. This felt good. I could really rest my weight on it. I experimented. 'If I lean really far forward, I can maybe swing my right leg without putting a lot of pressure on my foot as it touches the ground', I thought. 'Just kind of graze the concrete with my toes as I move the leg out of my hip, almost like a rudder...' I gave it a go.

Not too bad, actually. I mean - don't get me wrong - it felt ridiculous, and I'm sure it didn't look particularly graceful. It also gave me only an absolute minimum of forward movement, since I didn't use any real muscle power to push off, but - I moved. I tried the same technique a few more times. It was a fine line. My foot still connected and I wouldn't be able to do this excessively. But maybe I could do the same thing on the left? I tried, and I could. By pushing my right knee into the backpack and resting a maximum amount of weight on it, I could lean far forward - almost to the point that my torso was horizontal - and my rudder leg (I know) was now pushing *back* more so than down, which reduced the impact as it touched the ground.

Now - being the scooting equivalent of a swimmer in a neck brace and both arms in a cast - I was somehow making ground. After all I was still rolling, so I would hopefully be at least as fast as I would have been walking. But can you say 'back pain?'

By the time I reached Plymouth, IN - 19 miles after setting out that morning - I felt like someone had poured a gallon of lead into my lower back. My feet felt, well... not worse, I guess. It was hard to tell. But my body was screaming bloody murder at how I was treating it. I was utterly exhausted. I had decided to stop for late lunch in Plymouth - it was about 3:30 pm - and then hoped to be able to go another 25 miles to Warsaw, IN, and rest there for the night. I bought a sandwich, a yogurt and some fruit at a gas station and sat down on the curb outside. I had hoped for some real food at an actual restaurant, but everything was at least 0.2 miles out of the way, and any added distance was unacceptable at this point. Gas station food would have to do. I had also grabbed some ice and placed it on my shin to reduce the inflammation. I realized I was much hungrier than I thought as I began to eat and drink, and my body thanked me for the much needed nutrition. But something else became clear to me as I sat there under a - thankfully - cloudy sky: I had almost no strength left. I just couldn't talk away the fact that going another 25 miles with this 'human rudder' technique was borderline nuts. Ian's words came to mind: 'You have to call the shots, but we want you to make it all the way. If you have to use a bike, people will understand.' I tried to send my friends back home a picture of myself, sitting crumpled-up on the sidewalk. I wanted them to see how I looked. I needed someone to acknowledge how hard this was. The picture didn't go through. No service. T-Mobile had been the bane of my existence since about Arizona, and coverage would only get worse going East before it would get better. I felt disconnected - literally. Alone. Beat. I realized I wouldn't be able to keep going today. Not as far as Warsaw anyway, and that was where the next motel was. 'Damn it, I'm still losing miles every day', I thought. I used the calculator on my phone to find out what my average mileage going forward would be from here on out...Over 35. Jesus.

A teenage boy was driving circles on a nearby meadow with his screaming BMX motorcycle. I have sensitive hearing, it's been a thing all my life. The shrill sound penetrated my ears and it was detrimental to me in that moment, as I already felt buried under the weight of everything. I willed him to stop. 'Maybe if I send him a thousand yard stare he'll stop and move somewhere else?' I thought. Not a chance. He looked back defiantly and just kept going. I tried to stop hateful thoughts from forming in my mind: 'He's a kid', I berated myself. 'Give him a break, he's not doing it to upset you. Who knows what he has going on? Being a teenager is tough enough as it is, being a teenager in Plymouth, IN, probably doesn't help. It might be the only thing he's allowed to enjoy in his week.' In between all these thoughts I made the call: I would find a motel in Plymouth, and head for Warsaw the next day. It was still early, and I would get a good amount of rest, put up my legs - now plural - and ice them, hopefully healing them enough to improve the way I used the scooter. With the decision made I felt a weight off my back. Getting there was the most important thing. I had to choose my battles wisely to win the war, so to say.

I picked the *Days Inn* about a mile and a half away as my stop for the night. I could take my time now, and I was grateful for some short downhill stretches as I moved through different neighborhoods. Plymouth, IN, wasn't exactly a flourishing city. At least not the parts I came by. If it wasn't true poverty, it was certainly not what one would call a good standard of living most people enjoyed here. The old questions popped back into my head: why does everyone have to just scrape by? Why are houses and roads sub standard, cars old, public places not cared for and uninviting? Why did people not get the deal they deserved? I knew they worked hard. Almost everyone did. You should have a chance to enjoy your life if you worked 40 hours a week or more. Why were the economy and living standards for most people thriving in Denmark where they had a 35-hour work week, and everyone got to enjoy paid vacations and many months paid maternity leave? Why was that an unknown thing in the United States of America, where there was more money than anywhere else? Why did almost everyone have to be stressed out all the time, worried about their own and their children's future, weighed down by insane interest rates on their increasing debt, unable to live and love and laugh without the ever-nagging voice in the back of their minds that things were too tough to relax? All I could think was, that if I saw one more CEO talking about how a $15/hour minimum wage for their workers was unaffordable, while they raked in tens of millions of dollars annually, I would throw a fit. How could they be so arrogant to think their work was so goddamn important, that they deserved a thousand times the pay of their employees at the bottom of the chain? People who worked their butts off, under ridiculous corporate rules and regulations. And they'd better not complain or otherwise someone else desperate for a job would quickly fill their shoes. 'Yeah, a competitive environment, it's good for the economy!' some people will tell you. Please don't be one of them. People deserve and need a healthy, good standard of living. They need a break. They need joy and fun, and relaxation at regular intervals. They need plenty of time with their friends and families. They should have a chance to travel, and see the world. Experience art and culture. All that will contribute to their productivity at work. To say otherwise is corporate madness. All right, rant over.

After cursing out the Plymouth sidewalks for being as smooth as a bus ride in India - worsening my already borderline wrist situation - I checked in at the *Days Inn,* iced my legs and rested my tense lower back. I had put off informing the people following my journey on my page and on the *Bernie Sanders Activists* about my injuries and the scooter. I felt bad about spoiling the integrity

62

of my walk. I was afraid people wouldn't understand. But nothing could have been further from the truth: the feedback was overwhelmingly positive and reassuring. People told me I shouldn't risk permanent damage to my body, and accept rides from Bernie Sanders supporters along the way. They empathized with me, and told me they were behind me whatever was going to happen. So many expressed their appreciation for what I was doing. It made me feel better. I was probably being way too hard on myself: no one but I had determined the rules of this undertaking. No one but I decided what the integrity of it would stand or fall by. Only in my head had the idea taken hold that - since Bernie had built his life and political career on integrity and accountability - I had to be just as vigilant on my walk, since it symbolized his life's path for me.

That evening I was excited about having dinner at an actual restaurant. Overall, I tried to spend as little money as possible, in order to not go broke before actually making it to Philly, but I decided I had deserved this. I sat down in a nice little family restaurant. I had some spaghetti, and ice cream for desert. It was comforting to take part in a little social activity, even though I was on a table by myself. It still gave me a feeling of belonging. If nothing else, at least belonging to society in general. Because while traveling as I did, that sense wasn't present at all. I crossed paths with people frequently, of course. I passed them at gas stations, or they watched me cross an intersection through the windshield of their cars, probably curious to know why someone would trek along the Highway, and what was up with the Bernie T-shirt... But none of that gave me a feeling of being connected. I was *outside* whatever I was usually part of in life, and I would be until my journey was finished.

Weeks later I would walk through a charming lit up town on a Saturday night, feeling a bit like Emile Hirsch's character in 'Into the Wild' in the scene where he's looking through a bar window, watching as people enjoy their regular lives...

I relished my time at the restaurant, observing people. I wondered about the waiters, the guests entering and exiting. What were their lives like? Were they happy? Were they in love? Were they indifferent? Were they struggling? Did they know about the dire situation in many parts of the country? Were they aware of Bernie Sanders and his campaign platform?

I finished my food, paid and scooted back across the parking lot to my motel, which was maybe a hundred feet away. I always had the scooter with me. I didn't take a single step on my right foot if I could avoid it. I was on the road all day, and if I couldn't truly rest my foot to heal, I had to give it as much of a break as possible when the day was done.

Back in my room, I read a couple of pages in the only book I brought with me: the 'Tao Te Ching.' It was very thin and light. Lao Tzu's wisdom rings true today as much as it did 2,600 years ago in far away China. It soothed me to read a chapter or two before sleeping. I believe the Universe is truly unfathomable. That we're part of something bigger, something our intellect can't grasp. And that we can't control things. Sometimes it helps to just give in to that. To trust that things will work out. I tried to do that as I fell asleep...

Day 6 - planned destination: Columbia City, IN

I was up early the next day. I felt good after the longer turn around and knew I had made the right decision. Being rested would allow me to finally start catching up on miles, which I needed to start as soon as possible.

Warsaw, IN, was 26 miles away. I set my mind on making it there for a late lunch, and then hopefully reaching Columbia City after another 18 miles that night. It was a steep goal, considering how beat I was after going only 19 miles the day before. I googled the elevation of both Plymouth and Columbia City, hoping I would go downhill a lot. But there wasn't much of a difference, unfortunately.

Long stretches that day took me down the old Lincoln Highway, which was a welcome variation to the busy 30. As always there was a downside: there hadn't been a lot of rumble strips on the shoulder of the Highway recently, and the quality of the concrete had gotten better. Not so much on the old, less frequented Lincoln Highway: the quality of the road changed every few miles, and more than half of the time I had no choice but to walk on the side of the road, using the scooter as a crutch. There are about 4 or 5 different kinds of pavement that will vary depending on - to me - unknown factors, and I can safely say I am now an expert when it comes to the difference of experience in scooting on them (what a valuable thing to put on my resume).

I checked my phone during a short rest. My heart jumped as I saw that FBI director James Comey would make a public statement that day at 11am Eastern Standard Time, in all likelihood bringing to a close the year-long investigation regarding Hillary Clinton's private e-mail server. I couldn't get my pulse to slow down as I kept going. It was another hour until we would find out what his recommendation to the Department of Justice would be. Now, let me just say that I don't wish harm or misfortune on any living being. But I also believe in justice. And in the case of Hillary Clinton and her private server, where recklessness and complete disregard for important rules and laws was evident for everyone to see who was willing to see it, justice *needed* to be done. She was guilty, and we all knew it. James Comey knew it. He had studied the evidence for over a year. And as far as I could tell from doing a bit of research, the man was a model of integrity. After all, he had threatened a mass resignation of the FBI years earlier, should the DOJ not follow through on his recommendation to prosecute General Petraeus on a similar matter. Peanuts, really, compared to Hillary Clinton's case. 'She will get indicted', I reassured myself. 'There's no other way. And then Bernie will be the nominee. Basta.'

But I soon found out how far integrity goes in the political landscape of America today - it stops with Hillary Clinton, that much is certain. In his 15-minute speech James Comey told us exactly what we all knew already: She had violated the rules without regard for national security, possibly endangering American lives in the process, and all for her own convenience. And with no stretch of the imagination, to hide things from the public. And then, when we all were ready to celebrate the fact that real justice was alive and well in the US after all, director Comey ended with 'No criminal charges recommended for the former Secretary.' 'Wait, what? You just told us that she's guilty', I uttered in complete disbelief. My heart sank. What an illusion I had given myself to. I felt like a fool. I had actually believed that an independent organization like the FBI, lead by a badass such as James Comey, who prided himself on the credo that no one was above the law - *no one* - would actually follow through on recommending to indict one of the most powerful and connected political figures in America, if not the world. What was I thinking?

It was a brutal day for Bernie's movement. And not only for us. All across the country people were outraged. What do we have laws for, if there are no consequences for people who break them? Why should we believe anything after we're being lied to like this? Why believe in freedom and justice and democracy, when the government and agencies like the FBI clearly didn't operate by the same principles? I was so incredibly disappointed. The e-mail investigation was a pillar of hope. Now it was over, and nothing had changed. The chances for Bernie Sanders to still become the nominee had just dropped substantially, there was no denying that. 'I can't let it affect me', I told myself. I had to keep my hopes up, and believe there was a chance. My walk depended on it. How else would I be able to keep going? '*Something* will happen', I thought. 'Nothing is set in stone.'

Around 4pm I arrived in Warsaw. Warsaw, IN, is a charming city. But all I could think of was food and rest, and so I took in the town more in passing. One image did catch my attention, however: a warrior's memorial with the statues of Abraham Lincoln and another man beside it. The man holds a map and Lincoln takes him by the arm, seemingly explaining something to him (I would find out a couple of weeks down the line that this statue of Lincoln is a copy of the original, which stands in front of the David Wills house in Gettysburg):

I was tired, and really, really hungry. I needed a proper meal. I checked my phone for a restaurant that served hearty food and wasn't more than a few hundred feet out of my way, and dragged myself there.

I dropped my backpack and my scooter, and simply relished the feeling of sitting in a chair in an air conditioned room, before ordering a ham and cheese sandwich with fries and pickles. Anything tastes good when you're truly hungry, but good food is like a miracle. And this sandwich was perfection. I tried to not eat too fast and enjoy every bite, but I also couldn't linger for too long. A half hour to forty minute break would have to do. I was never not aware, that the additional 18 miles I had yet to put in would take everything out of me, and I couldn't get back on the road too late.

I don't remember much about the rest of the way, other than that it was tough. But also picturesque and beautiful. The corn fields glowed golden from the low hanging sun, and the sight made up for drivers honking at me for using the scooter on *their* road:

I reached Columbia City just before 10pm. I was completely spent. This gorgeous sunset lifted my spirits enough to look forward with some optimism:

There were several motels in a half mile radius. The cheapest one was the *Budget Inn*, and that's where I decided to go. I fought my way across a gravel mine field of a parking lot, cursing impatiently as the scooter got stuck over and over again, before I finally stood in the tiny little office and asked for a room. I deflated when the owner told me their credit card machine was broken - he would only accept cash. It meant I had to drag the scooter through the gravel once again, then head back up the hill to squeeze $60 out of the ATM at Walgreens. But since the motel didn't have an ice machine, I had to go anyway. I desperately needed to ice my shins and feet. After finding a helpful video online earlier, I had taped up my shins on both sides, which helped a lot. The inflammation was about 50% reduced on the right side, and - after feeling troubling first symptoms on my left over the last days - that side hadn't gotten worse either.

My room was simple and clean, and I liked it. I also felt like the owner had made an effort to make me feel comfortable, which is not to be taken for granted for a man who has the sobering task of dealing with complete strangers traveling through every day.

I bathed. I had bought more epsom salt at the Walgreens. It helped soothe my muscles and smelled of Eucalyptus. I used it as often as I could. The only problem was that epsom salt is only available in large packs at any Walgreens, CVS or Rite Aid. After using some of it, I was left with a bag that weighed 3 or 4 pounds, which I simply couldn't take with me in my backpack. So I got into the habit of taking as much as I could carry with me, and pouring the rest into the trash.

I was sad that night. No doubt the exhaustion I felt after traveling 45 miles the way I did, played a part. But sadness is sadness. It didn't matter why I felt it. I missed my (ex)fiancee, my home, my cats. I missed Los Angeles, and everything that was my life there. I cried for a long time. I was in some motel right alongside a busy highway in the middle of Indiana, unsure how much farther I was going to make it with the state I was in, and if this whole thing was maybe just a giant mistake. A short circuit in my idealistic mind. Arrogance. Desperation... 'Is there really still a chance for Bernie Sanders to become President?' I thought. What was I doing here? What was I fighting for? In that moment, really all that evening, I'm not sure I remembered. I just waited till the tears dried on my cheeks, and sleep overcame me...

Day 7 - planned destination: New Haven, IN

After leaving the motel the next morning I stocked up on Gatorade and energy bars at the Walgreens up the road. I hadn't been able to shake my sadness. I felt a deep emptiness inside me, and I felt alone out here. The thought of doing this every day, all day long, for nearly three more weeks was depressing and overwhelming. It seemed too difficult. Too burdensome. I felt incredibly heavy.

At least the distance wasn't as daunting that day: 28 miles to New Haven, IN. So I remembered the credo that would become my most essential tool for making it to the end: one step at a time, and at some point it will be over.

I spent almost the entire way from Columbia City to New Haven on the shoulder of the 30 Highway. If I remember correctly, that was also the day when rumble strips returned with a vengeance. It was so frustrating to not be able to scoot on the shoulder, I actually went out on the road several times when there was a gap in traffic (just to be clear: the 30 in that area is a large and busy highway, so that was no joke). I knew it wasn't sensible, and if police had spotted me there would have been no way around a ticket. But I didn't have a choice.

When I checked my phone somewhere along the way I was very excited to find that - after she saw my post in the *Bernie Sander Activists* Facebook group - a generous lady, her name was Crimson, offered to put me up for the night in New Haven. I private messaged her, and we arranged a meeting point.

Meanwhile my path finally took me off the 30 and onto smaller roads, as I was heading for Fort Wayne:

(I pushed as much as I could to get used to walking again)

I had heard of Fort Wayne, IN, but didn't know anything more about it than the name. It was certainly larger than any city I had seen in a while. I went past a cemetery that caught my eye, since literally every name on the tombstones was German. I mean *every single one*. It made me wonder about the history of the city and - sure enough - a bit of research confirmed that at the turn of the 20th century a huge number of German immigrants settled there. So it was a bit like riding my scooter through home turf. New Haven is more or less a suburb of Fort Wayne, and after a few more miles I reached the intersection where Crimson and I had agreed to meet. The sun was about to set, and I sat myself down on a curb outside a bank. It was quiet around me. Almost no traffic, and not many people about. The air had cooled down, the temperature was perfect. I enjoyed not having to move, and I let myself be at ease. Just taking in the moment.

After about twenty minutes a gold Pontiac Grand Am pulled up in the parking lot, and Crimson and her daughter Tawnie got out. I waved, and Crimson smiled and walked toward me. 'You're real!' I joked. 'And I'm gross, by the way.' She hugged me anyway. It felt good to connect with someone after being alone all day. Tawnie gave me a hug as well, and granddaughter Blaire shyly said hello through the backseat window. Every time I got to meet someone who had reached out to help me, it warmed my heart. And Crimson and Tawnie were wonderful people, I felt that right away. After Crimson expressed concern over my health - it wasn't lost on her that I moved like an old man - we went for dinner.

Little Blaire remained shy for a bit, but soon we had lots of fun while dining on spaghetti, garlic bread and soda. Children are incredible, the way they soak up everything like a sponge - you think they're not paying attention, but nothing gets lost. I asked Crimson to tell me a bit about herself. Crimson wasn't her real first name, but it had stuck from her job in the music industry, where she worked on and off as an event organizer. It wasn't her only job - she maintained machinery at McDonald's, and the next morning her shift would start at 5am. She made no secret out of the fact that she didn't enjoy it, but it wasn't easy to make ends meet these days. Tawnie, who worked at the same McDonald's, had planned for me to spend the night in her basement, but it was so hot she said it would be unbearable without air conditioning, and she and Crimson insisted to pay for a motel for me. I said I understood about the room and that I would gladly pay for the motel myself, but they insisted. I accepted, humbled and moved by their generosity. $50 is a lot of money when you're just getting by. I know the feeling. We finished dinner, and headed out.

On the way to the motel, Crimson and Tawnie educated me about the huge drug problem New Haven - and Fort Wayne, for that matter - had. It was an epidemic really. Predominantly Meth, but also Heroin and Cocaine, had many - especially young - people, addicted. Some of Tawnie's friends were among them, and I couldn't help but notice the sadness and defeat in her voice as she told me some stories: one of her friends, a young guy with a promising future in skateboarding, had gotten badly hurt at *one of those* parties: there had been a fight, probably over a girl. The other man had walked to his car, returned with a crowbar and bashed Tawnie's friend's head in with it. Then he grabbed a box cutter and slashed open the palms of his hands, as he was lying there unconscious. Tawnie's friend survived, but his dreams of a skateboarding career are over. The doctor told him should he fall and hit his head, he could die.

It was just one tragic case out of many, and Indiana wasn't the only state in the US that was experiencing drug epidemics, either. And it wasn't an accident that the situation was getting worse parallel to the larger picture in the country. These people were looking for an escape in a time when there seemed to be no path forward. No future. No opportunities. Where they saw all around them that it didn't matter how hard you worked: you would always struggle, while a powerful few were swimming in wealth. Bernie had addressed this issue at every rally. He knew it was pressing, and he cared.

We reached the motel. Crimson and Tawnie accompanied me to the office and paid for the room. Again, I felt a sting in my chest. 'Is it right for me to accept their offer?' I worried. 'Will I be the reason Tawnie has to think twice next time she wants to take Blaire to the movies?' When we said goodbye Crimson invited me to come for breakfast at her McDonald's the next morning. Tawnie would pick me up at 9am. I gladly accepted. We said good night, and they left.

I was completely spent. I remember clearly how low I felt that night. Despite the great company - or maybe because of it. These kind women's stories of struggle and hardship, youth around here battling drug addiction, the people I'd seen hanging out in front of the motel, their faces marked by addiction, and the overall look and feel of New Haven, IN, which was another example of a struggling and crumbling city in the US, had me in its grasp. I felt incredibly cut off from the world and everything I knew. It all seemed hopeless. When I finally couldn't resist anymore what felt like a gaping hole inside me, I broke into tears and couldn't stop crying - once again. At some point I fell asleep.

I was still exhausted the next morning when Tawnie and Blaire picked me up. I wondered if they could sense how heavy I felt. How drained. We headed to McDonald's where I was greeted by Crimson. She had finished her shift early, and came out to join us:

(Crimson and Tawnie with Blaire)

I was treated to breakfast, and enjoyed every bite of it. I didn't have long before I needed to head out, and it made me sad that I

76

had to rush my time with this lovely family. I handed Crimson a few things that I had decided weighed my backpack down unnecessarily - among them my Kindle, which I had brought as a backup device to document everything in case my phone broke - and asked her if she would mind sending me a package back to LA at some point. She said it wasn't a problem at all and I gave her $12, which I hoped would cover the cost.

We finished breakfast, then Crimson, Tawnie and Blaire drove me back to the spot they picked me up at the night before. We hugged goodbye. I could tell Crimson was worried about me. She knew I had 45 miles ahead of me that day, and she had seen my limp and the effort it took me to get out of the car. I reassured her I would be fine. I didn't know I would be, honestly. But I could only find out by heading on.

I watched them drive off as we waved goodbye. The way they had taken care of me had left an impact. A part of me didn't want them to go. They'd given me comfort, and now I was alone again. I took a deep breath, fastened my backpack and set out.

Day 8 - planned destination: Kalida, OH

It was another one of those long stretches on the shoulder of the 30 Highway for the first miles that day. I tried to scoot as much as I could, since I had a ton of ground to cover. But the constant push off motion wore me out. It's hard enough to do this all day, but when you can feel time breathing down your neck it makes it that much harder.

It began to drizzle. I put my phone away so it wouldn't get wet, and when I looked at the screen realized I had just crossed into Ohio. I was ecstatic, and here's why: I had told myself at some point that if I made it to Ohio, I could make it to Pennsylvania. And once I crossed into Pennsylvania, nothing was going to stop me. Those were hypotheticals, of course. I could have been forced to stop for many reasons in either state. But you need those markers in your head, and one of them I had just put behind me. Yes!

I'd been on the road for about 15 miles when I scooted off the 30, and onto the 12, a quiet countryside Highway. I stopped and took in the far reaching land in front of me. A combine harvester made its rounds on a golden hay field to my left:

'This is exactly how I pictured Ohio', I thought, then checked the map on my phone. I did a double take as I noticed that the rest of the way to Kalida, OH - almost 30 miles - was one long straight, except for the last tiny bit that veered off into the town center. I remembered well how tough the 11-mile straight into Valparaiso was... 'Holy cow, hopefully this won't be as bad', I thought. I don't know if you have a route familiar to you that's about that distance (for me it's approximately West Hollywood to San Pedro). If you do, try to imagine it as one long straight: no turns. No bends in the road. No large intersections. No traffic lights. Only fields and the occasional tree alongside. A farm or residence every mile or so. Barely cars. Now imagine already having 15 miles in your legs when that straight opens before you... Thank God the Earth's surface curves out of sight at a distance of approximately 3 miles, otherwise I probably would have dropped everything right then and there.

After a few minutes on the 12 I felt a concern growing in the back of my mind: water. I checked the route again and found no gas stations or stores anywhere near my path for the next twenty miles. I still had a bottle and a half of Gatorade, but that wouldn't last me very long. Temperatures were in the 80s in the shade, and

I would be exposed to the sun basically the entire time. I considered my options as I passed a lone house, about a hundred feet to my right. A man was working on his car in the open garage. I decided to give it a shot - it couldn't hurt. I headed in his direction, waving. When he finally saw me I asked if I could fill up my hydration pack, since I had a long way ahead of me and little water left. He generously offered for me to come inside, to be out of the sun for a minute. The man's wife introduced herself to me as he filled up my pack with cold water. Their three dogs eyed me carefully and curiously. One was jumpy and nervous, and the couple told me that he was a rescue, who had been mistreated by his former male owner. For a split second I felt hot anger over the cruel treatment some animals are exposed to by humans. Then it was replaced by the reassuring feeling that this dog was now safe, and in good hands. 'So you're a Bernie Sanders fan?' the man asked me, as he handed me my filled hydration pack, simultaneously pointing at my T-shirt. I smiled, and explained what I was doing. They looked at me incredulously, and it lead to a fifteen minute conversation about politics, in which they revealed - as almost everyone did who I crossed paths with on my journey - that they disliked and distrusted Hillary Clinton with a passion. We could have talked forever, and I did my best to give my view on the many advantages of a Bernie Sanders presidency, but then I needed to say goodbye. I was running out of time with nearly 28 miles left to go. 'It was a good idea to fill up on water', they told me. 'There's nothing out there for a long time.' I thanked them, and set out to the excited barking of their dogs.

I treasure this random encounter. These people and I had little in common, given where and how they lived versus my own life situation, and they were definitely Republican in their beliefs. But I felt taken care of by them. They had invited me into their home and made sure I was safe, with plenty of water for the way. Kindness, born from compassion toward another human being. It lifted my spirits. Later on I would think of them every time I held the frozen water bottle they had given me in addition to my neck -

it was bliss. But there was one thing I couldn't get over, no matter how good it felt: the straight never ended...

It's tough on the mind, I've said it before. Something happens when there's no change of direction. No turning a corner. No little goals to check off and say *on to the next one*. It does funny things to you. Naturally, I was always heading East, so later in the afternoon the sun was low behind me. I could feel it blasting onto my back, and lighting up the corn and hay fields left and right of me. Everything was dipped into a dark golden color. I was completely alone out here on this road. Every fifteen minutes or half an hour a car passed, but that was it. There was nothing but me and my shadow extending before me on the concrete:

I stopped and took it in. It's a curious thing how sunlight creates this cutout of you. In a way your shadow seems to stand out from the lit ground around it, but if you look at it a different way it's more like your body creates a sort of hole. You're the nonentity. Everything *is* around you. Only that silhouette created by your physical form *isn't*.

I'm getting more philosophical about it now than I was in the moment. Out there the experience at hand was too powerful to distract myself with elaborate thoughts. And sometimes I wished I could have escaped that way. To just go off into my thoughts or imagination. To not feel the arduousness of the task. But too much thinking weighed me down more than anything, and so there was no other way than to simply deal with it.

The road never seemed to end.

A little later, during a quick rest, I was shocked to find that - on top of the challenge at hand - I had overlooked something: earlier that day I had googled the motel/hotel situation for Kalida, OH, and found several options. 'No need to reserve ahead of time', I had thought. Now, as I wanted to determine my exact destination for the night, I realized that what I had seen were motels *in the area*, not the town itself: there was no hotel, motel or bed & breakfast within 20 miles of Kalida. I tried not to let anxiety get the better of me, but the fact was that all of a sudden I was in the middle of nowhere and had no place to stay for the night. Worse, I wouldn't get to Kalida before 10pm. So even if there was a samaritan hiding out somewhere, possibly offering me their garage or something like that as a roof over my head - which was a far stretch of the imagination to begin with - the restaurants and public places where I would be able to talk to people would all close soon... 'Take a breath', I told myself, and I remembered that thousands of Bernie supporters were only a Facebook post away. Maybe there was someone in the area who could give me a place to sleep. Or at least pick me up in Kalida and drop me off at the closest motel.

I was nervous, I'm not going to lie. But not long after I posted my request - or plea, really - a woman told me she lived in Lima,

OH, which was about 20 miles away. She said she would have me stay at her place, but her dogs would be an issue. I assured her that giving me a ride to a motel in Lima would be epically helpful to me. She said she'd be happy to do that, and I should let her know once I was 20 minutes away from Kalida town center. 'Good God, thank you', I whispered. I felt such gratitude toward this woman, and I hadn't even met her yet. But Kalida was still a ways to go, and the 12 seemed to extend farther and farther out the longer I travelled on it.

By the time evening fell, every minute seemed to last three times its length. This sunset made me forget everything for a moment...

...but soon after I had given up hoping I would come to the end of this road. It just wouldn't happen. I was toast. Utterly exhausted. Even when I saw I had almost reached the turn heading into town - and thus, only a few miles left - I couldn't imagine where to take the strength from. Again, time seemed to stand still. I didn't seem to move. But night came over me all the same, and once more I was faced with being in the dark at the end of a long, exhausting and painful journey.

And then I was saved by fireflies... At first I only saw a glimpse here and there. But soon more and more began to light up on the neatly trimmed lawns outside the first houses I passed. I stopped in awe. It was delightful. What beauty! Dozens and dozens of the little creatures switched on their lamps at the same time, turning this hauntingly still night into a fairy tale landscape (it was too dark for pictures, unfortunately). Imagine a kid walking along, eyes large and mouth wide open. That was me. I didn't know if to look to the left or right side of the road, because they were everywhere. It sounds cheesy, but I want to say my soul smiled. We all know mind, body and spirit work together - I don't need to tell you that. But what a perfect example this was for how an exhausted body and mind can be revived by the wonder and beauty of nature. And so I went on with a little more ease in my movements, and - literally - lighter inside.

Around 10:30 I finally reached the town center of Kalida. I had let Erin - the lady who would come to pick me up - know that I was close, and she was on her way. The town was tiny. No wonder they had no hotels around here. It was very quiet. Orange light from a few street lamps made the unfamiliar surroundings look a little less strange and foreign. I saw a pizza place that still had its lights on, and I was more than mildly excited when I found that it was indeed still open. I couldn't wait to get some real food in me.

After ordering, I limped to the bathroom. Slow and careful. I had asked a lot of my body that day, and I didn't need any additional pain or injuries.

When I came back I found Erin and her son CeyShon waiting for me. Actually, at first glance I wasn't sure what their relationship was: Erin is white and CeyShon black. Erin looked way younger than her age, and CeyShon was tall and had a powerful presence about him, and I would have definitely estimated him older than he really was, which was 16. So my first thought was that they were friends, or even a couple. But soon I learned that CeyShon was Erin's son. We said hello, neither of us totally comfortable with this unusual situation. I felt embarrassed about how dirty and sweaty I was, and I'm sure I didn't smell that great from up close. But they reassured me it was not an issue, and - since my food had just arrived - I asked them to join me before setting out.

We munched on pizza, as I expressed my gratitude for what they were doing for me. Erin was very politically interested and engaged, and a hardcore Bernie supporter. And she had her personal reasons: she had recently taken in her mother to live with her, CeyShon and her husband, since her mother couldn't make it on her own with the minimal social security money she received each month. One of Bernie Sanders' most important platform issues was to expand social security, so people who retired wouldn't have to live on $11,000 or less a year, which was simply not possible. But hearing about real individual fates suddenly makes the matter a hundred times clearer: Erin's mother received $700/month social security. And after health care co-payments and deductibles she was left with even less - just over $500. So Erin had no choice but to take her in.

CeyShon, who played football for a local high school team among other things, was taken with what I was doing. I could see him paying rapt attention as I was describing details of my journey. He was a young man itching for adventure. I really enjoyed his enthusiasm. And there was something else about him... He seemed more aware than the average teenager. There was a bright light on in his eyes. He was open, soaking things in. I knew immediately that Erin and his Dad had done a great job raising him.

It got past 11pm, and it was time to drive to Lima and get to my motel. But that meant I had to get up and walk. Resting and eating had made me realize how spent I was, and now every movement required monumental effort. It was as if my limbs were made of concrete. I felt so old and worn out. 'How am I going to keep doing this for another two weeks?' I thought to myself.

CeyShon sat in the back next to me as Erin drove us through pitch black rural Ohio. I could feel his restlessness. His excitement. He told me he would like nothing more than to accompany me, at least for a day. Until the next stop or so. I smiled. I hadn't even considered anything of that sort, but it warmed my heart that this young man liked and trusted me enough to want to join me for a part of my journey. Erin quickly made it clear that wasn't realistic, and I had to agree: walking on the highway wasn't exactly safe to begin with, and - even if we would make it to the next stop without issues - CeyShon would have to get back to Lima somehow. Erin and his father had to work, and public transport in this area...well, you can imagine.

We reached the *Motel 6* I had reserved a room at, and Erin invited me to join her and CeyShon for breakfast the next morning at the restaurant she worked at, which was close by. I happily agreed, glad to not have to say goodbye right away.

Once in my room, I quickly turned to nursing my body by taking a hot bath and icing my legs afterward. I had given up on discerning between which area got the ice treatment. It was whatever parts had hurt throughout the day, or were hurting now - which was everything from the knees down. I had zero strength left after the 45 miles I had put behind me. Every day my turnaround time was under 12 hours, and it simply wasn't enough to recuperate sufficiently. I watched a few minutes of TV to shoo away my worries and doubts, and then went to sleep. Hoping the coming night would somehow magically last for 20 hours...

When I opened my eyes the next morning, I knew right away that the night had been exactly as long as any before or after (shouldn't there be the option of having a magic wish granted every once in a while?). Well, as it was - in the real world - I was still beat when I got up.

Erin and CeyShon picked me up and we soon took our seats in the busy restaurant. Erin's colleagues served us, and I relished my coffee and eggs with grits on the side. I'm probably repeating myself, but after a daily diet of energy bars, bananas, Gatorade and the occasional gas station sandwich, every bite of *real* food was incredibly precious to me. Erin and CeyShon agreed to let me film them as they talked a bit about the political race and - among other things - the current situation regarding police violence toward Black people. CeyShon turned very still and serious when he revealed that fear of law enforcement was not unknown to him as a young Black man in the Midwest, and that it weighed heavily on him to see that there was a not so low chance that the color of his skin could get him hurt or killed. Erin told me later that she had to hold back the tears hearing this. She had never had this conversation with CeyShon, and it made her incredibly sad to know he felt - or was forced to feel - that way.

After breakfast we drove back to Kalida town center, where I had stopped the night before. We took some pictures together, laughing and joking around, simply having a great time:

Once again, saying goodbye wasn't easy. Bernie supporters were in this fight for a better and fairer America together, and it bonded us. You didn't need to be related or know each other for long to feel like you had much in common. I wanted to give CeyShon something meaningful on his way... Something to convey that I knew he had huge potential, and that great things were ahead of him. I don't know what I ultimately said, but it wasn't necessary: I believe he could feel it without me telling him. Erin had been so generous and supportive. I gave her a big hug, thanking her for all she had done for me. I counted myself lucky to have met - yet again - such wonderful people. I think all of us knew that this encounter would stay with us. We smiled and laughed, waving goodbye as the two drove off and soon disappeared around the corner. And I was on to another day on the road...

Weeks later, back in California, I saw on Facebook that CeyShon was protesting at a rally of Mike Pence (at that time Donald Trump's vice president pick) and was removed from the venue by security. I was proud of him. He was being an activist. He was standing up for himself and the Black community. I wish I had had that strength of character as a teenager.

Day 9 - planned destination: Findlay, OH

Some of the traveling becomes a bit of a blur in my memory. Generally, my average day consisted of scooting on the shoulder of the busy 30; stretches here and there on the old Lincoln Highway, with less traffic but more walking due to bad roads; frequent breaks for Gatorade and water, and to nibble on energy bars or bananas; stops at gas stations to stock up on said supplies, and usually one longer break which I would use to ice my legs and eat something more substantial - though still gas station food. But I think day 9 took me down the old Highway a lot, looking at the photos I took:

What I do remember very clearly was the juxtaposition of the incredibly gorgeous view around me as I was coming through the outskirts of Findlay, OH, with an almost otherworldly bright golden sun setting over the land, and experiencing some of the most frustrating miles of this entire journey. The road was smooth enough, and from what I could tell Findlay was pretty. To top it off, the last stretch to my destination was heading downhill, and so this ride might have been almost pleasant. But the shoulder on both sides was so narrow that I was blocking traffic if I tried to scoot along, and beside it there was nothing but soil and gravel. I got honked at several times - for good reason - and eventually felt too unsafe to keep going. So I had to walk. Which was twice as hard knowing I had to put weight on my still injured foot for a long stretch, and that I could have rolled downhill had there been any goddamn space! I wanted to pull my hair out, it was so frustrating.

I finally arrived at the *Econo Lodge* to an incredible last phase of the sunset. Despite being completely spent I couldn't help but take pictures as the sky turned pink and orange above me:

It created a strange atmosphere. Foreboding. Like Ragnarök, the Twilight of the Gods in Nordic Mythology. The end of civilization... I'm sure I projected my inner state on to it. Somebody else might have felt happy looking heavenward. But my mood was as low as it had ever been. Feeling physically drained left me without any defenses against emotions bubbling up inside. I was missing my friends, and my former partner. My life back home.

I got to my room. The *Econo Lodge* was a little more upscale than some of the other motels - there was simply no cheaper option available that night. I needed food before I could take care of nursing my body with a hot bath. The motel was right by a large highway intersection, and there was a gas station about 0.2 miles away on the other side. There was no sidewalk to get across. Lots of places in America's midland aren't built for pedestrians, and this was one of them. I walked across, anyway. I'm not sure why I didn't use the scooter, but if I remember correctly my wrists were in disconcertingly bad shape (I couldn't hold a fork or knife anymore at this point, just to give you an idea) and I hoped walking on the grass at the side of the highway wouldn't do too much damage to my legs. Once again, pre packed gas station food was going to be my dinner. I felt so utterly out of place. Everything was concrete, loud engines and florescent light. And beyond the concrete nothing but large fields. And beyond them more fields. My only company my aching body, and a sky painted with my heartache. I don't know when I've ever felt this alone.

Day 10 - planned destination: Tiffin, OH

The next day the world seemed better as I made my way out of Findlay. The sun was shining, and I knew I had slightly less than my average miles - 25 to be precise - to go until my next stop. It wasn't my choice to lose miles again, but this was one of those times where finding a motel along the path ahead was a challenge, and I had to take a slight detour through a town called Tiffin. 'It will allow me to take it a bit easier', I reassured myself.

I passed a drawing of the Statue of Liberty on a brick wall. I took a picture and shared it with Bernie supporters on Facebook with this caption:

Goodbye, Findlay, OH. May this drawing be a good omen - for liberty and justice to prevail:

Shortly after two young men approached me. They were dressed in the same clothes - slacks and white button down shirt - and wore a name tag. They were young, early 20s maybe, and seemed open and friendly. I was curious about their names. 'Elder Beavers' and 'Elder Burr' it read on the name tags, and they agreed to tell me on camera about their tradition: *Elder* means teacher in Hebrew, and both of them would be traveling around Ohio for two years to pass on their church's teaching. In exchange I told them about my own quest. They hadn't heard of Bernie Sanders, or any of the other candidates, for that matter. Which was understandable. I had never given a rat's ass about politics myself until a year prior, and I on the other hand knew nothing about their religion. But I felt a kinship with them. We were all out here for something we believed in wholeheartedly.

After a few minutes we wished each other all the best for the journey ahead. Elder Beavers and Elder Burr were still young, but sincere about their task - I could see it in their eyes - and that's a precious thing. It's why they stayed with me, and will always have a warm place in my memory of my walk:

(Elder Beavers and Elder Burr)

I reached Tiffin, OH, at around 7pm. I was so tired. Underneath my resolve to make it to Philadelphia and keep fighting for the movement, there was dread over my physical state and profound exhaustion. Every now and again someone warned me of doing permanent damage to my body in the comments to one of my posts. And while I tried to disregard these well-intentioned messages, they stuck in the back of my mind. The truth is, I couldn't know for sure that I wasn't endangering my health. 'One day at a time', I reminded myself. 'One day at a time.'

My motel was right behind a Denny's and so I decided to get some dinner there. The staff saw my T-shirt and my scooter, and they were curious to find out what I was doing. And so I told them. The manager, a Republican, looked at me in disbelief.

When she found out that I wasn't even an American citizen but only a permanent resident, she interrupted me: 'Wait a second, you're walking from Chicago to Philadelphia to help fix the political system so Americans will have a better future, and you're not even American?' 'Yes', I gave back. Without hesitation she reached inside a drawer, and handed me a coupon for a free breakfast the next morning. I was so moved by this. I smiled and said thank you, hugged her, and then hobbled out with my pasta and garlic bread.

Day 11 - planned destination: Willard, OH

The next morning, after enjoying my breakfast at Denny's - in between munching on delicious eggs and hash browns I had kept looking around the room, hoping people wouldn't notice my dirty clothes - I set out with newfound optimism. The more days went by on this journey, the more I realized the magical power of the sun: at night everything seemed hopeless, pointless and insurmountable. But day light diminished pain and worries like no medicine could. At least for the first stretch...

After a few hours of scooting/walking through rural Ohio, I passed a house to my left, and at the same time noticed a dark lump on the road further ahead. 'Roadkill', I knew. 'Probably a raccoon.' Nothing surprising at this point. As I came closer I realized the animal was a different color than that of a raccoon. 'Oh no, a cat', I thought, and soon my fears were confirmed. She was pretty. Fully grown, with a nice ginger coat. She definitely had an owner. No stray cat looks this well groomed and well fed. She had no visible injuries, just some blood gathered around her mouth. Her tongue was sticking out, and her limbs had already stiffened slightly. 'She probably got hit in the head by a car', I theorized. Her body was still warm, so it couldn't have been that long ago. My heart sank. I have two cats. Their names are Zelda and Luna and they are like children to me. The thought alone of something like this happening to them was painful.

My eyes wandered back to the property I had just walked past. I remembered there was a cardboard cut out of a cat right next to the mailbox, signaling that a cat lived there. 'She must be their's', I thought. I dropped my scooter and my backpack in the grass and picked up the cat. It was a strange feeling. She was heavy. And some part of me was expecting her to come back to life. Through the trees I saw a lady hanging up laundry in the garden. I called out to her as I walked in her direction, almost ceremoniously carrying the ginger in my hands. 'Is this your cat?' I asked. 'I found her on the road.' The lady looked over, trying to figure out what was going on. Then she headed toward me. She was in her late 50s with a kind face and the stern eyes and tough features of someone who has seen a lot in life. 'Oh no, my Ally', she said, and then gently took the cat out of my hands. 'I've had her since she was a kitten.' I tried not to cry as I watched her stroke Ally's fur, but - as you know by now - I wasn't exactly tough and strong during those days. I blurted out how sorry I was for her loss. That I had cats, too, and how precious they were to me. The lady took it in. I could tell she appreciated my empathy. 'She's still warm', she said. 'It must have happened not too long ago. Where did you find her?' I pointed to the area on the road where I'd spotted Ally, and the lady sighed knowingly. 'Yes, that's where she went to see her chipmunk friend', she told me. I couldn't hold in my tears anymore, and - seeing that she was quietly crying herself - I hugged her. She let it happen. When we let go, she looked at me and I felt there was a sense of gratitude in her eyes. 'I can only imagine what you're feeling right now', I told her. 'I wish there was something I could do.' She smiled sadly, and I realized that nothing I could say would make her experience any better or any less sad. She was holding the body of a little being she had cared for and shared her life with for many years. For all I knew this felt like the death of a family member to her. So I just stood with her for a few more moments as we mourned Ally's demise together, and then I said goodbye.

I turned around, and headed back. I had snot running down my nose and tears flowing like rivers before I even reached my backpack and scooter. I walked on, unable to control my grief. This was one of the saddest things I ever had to do, and under the circumstances it completely overwhelmed me.

It took close to an hour for the sting to go away, and for the tears to stop coming. I somehow felt like I had discovered another level of emotional depth within me through this event, and - since I tried to document my experience as honestly as possible - I shared it on my page, together with this picture:

Once again many people related and shared their thoughts and feelings in the comment section. It seemed that whenever I expressed honest emotions - as I had done with my first post after the California election - there was a recognition, an appreciation, and it struck a chord with people. I guess when we show how we truly feel others recognize themselves in us. When the front we put up is dropped, and only the most human core remains, there is nothing that separates us from the other. Underneath we're all the same. The same fears, the same needs, the same emotions. It was encouraging to think about this as I headed on, and I remembered that Senator Sanders' response to the question which quality of character he would like to be remembered for if he became president was: *compassion*. Wasn't this what had happened between me and the lady who lost Ally? Wasn't this exactly why I was out here? Wasn't it precisely what Bernie attempted to tell us in every speech - that we have to learn again to *care for each other?* It made so much sense. The beauty in fighting for Bernie Sander's platform was that it had nothing much to do with politics as America and much of the world has come to understand it. It was about humanity! It was about taking care of all the members within a community. It was about *loving thy neighbor as thyself*, to put it in the words of good old Jesus. How could we not fight with every fiber of our being for the opportunity to have a man who really understood and embodied this truth to be our president? Not to mention with a wonderful woman by his side - Jane Sanders, who I couldn't wait to refer to as the first lady - who lived and breathed the same values? We couldn't, was the answer. And I was going to do everything in my power to help them get there. Even if my efforts were but a drop on a hot stone.

I reached Willard, OH, later that day:

The place looked familiar somehow, and I believe I came through here in 2009 when I drove cross country on my move from New York to Los Angeles. Willard is not exactly the most picturesque town in the US. It's a place people come through - just like I had - and it had little more to offer than fast food chains, motels, pharmacies and auto shops. Not a lot of history, culture, or art. I stopped at a CVS to get Gatorade for the next day, and a bag of epsom salts. My hot bath with eucalyptus or lavender scent had become one of the things I looked forward to most in my day.

I found the *Country Hearth Inn,* my motel for the night, at the other end of town, a few hundred feet to the left of the Highway. It had a huge, open lawn in the back, and the rooms were spacious. I felt very comfortable there. And since my journey that day had only been a little under 27 miles (which meant I had arrived while it was still light out) I got a couple of extra hours to enjoy it. Unfortunately, I subsequently would have a whole lot more ground to cover the day after: 47 miles to Wooster, OH. That's a stretch, even with using the scooter. So I rested and relaxed as much as I could while watching TV, and then I went to sleep early.

Day 12 - planned destination: Wooster, OH

Setting out the next morning, I soon saw the first signs lining the road that described Civil War areas and events along my path (this would, of course, continue all throughout the state of Pennsylvania later on). One of those signs I saw in Shiloh, OH:

I also passed several horse carriages, steered by Amish men and women. This self-serve straw shed and the for-sale horse carriage epitomize what the land and towns I came through that day looked and felt like. Very rural (an unusual sight for someone living in Los Angeles, CA):

As a side note I want to say that - knowing nothing about the Amish, and never before having met anyone of that culture/religion - every single encounter with them was friendly and pleasant.

I knew I had a long way to go and I spent as much time on the scooter as I could that day. So you'll understand how frustrated I was when roads like these didn't seem to end:

I vividly remember how every hit from tears in the concrete or potholes or gravel hurt my wrists that day. The continued shocks to my already tender joints worried and angered me. I felt torn. I knew I had to keep up the pace to make the distance, but I also knew I'd injure myself sooner or later if I kept going like this. At some point I simply lost it. I threw the scooter into the grass and tore my backpack off my shoulders, steaming with anger. This was impossible! I sat down on an embankment, trying to calm myself and catch my breath. After a while I looked to my left, and what I saw made my frustration evaporate. There it was again, the magic number:

'I guess I'm on the right way', I chuckled to myself.

I continued on, having given up hope for anything resembling a smooth road that day, when at some point Google maps told me to turn left at an intersection. I was now a little less than 3 miles away from my destination of Wooster, OH, and the concrete on this new road was simply perfect: freshly paved, black, smooth asphalt - and it lead downhill. Had I died and gone to Heaven? I didn't want to get too excited, at first. Maybe the concrete would be edgy and rough again around the next bend, or the path would lead uphill for the last 2 miles into town. But soon I was rolling down a wide and empty road with the sun setting in my back, like I was living a young boy's summer evening fantasy. Oh, if I could describe to you the joy I felt in that moment... The valley Wooster was nestled in opened up before me as I sped downhill at close to 30mph for what must have been a half mile or more, and not a single car or truck passed me during the entirety of my kamikaze thrill ride! I laughed and yelled and howled like a wolf, relishing the experience with all my senses. Throughout this whole journey a part of me had constantly held watch in the back of my head to remind me that this walk was not for my own personal pleasure, and - if anything - it should be hard and difficult, not enjoyable. But in this moment I let that go. The last twelve days had not been easy. I decided that I deserved to have a little fun. And God is my witness, I had the time of my life during those few minutes.

Actually, it turned out I was having a bit too much fun: when the road ended at an intersection in the valley, I barely was able to stop the scooter (the break is a simple block of rubber you step on to slow the back wheel, and it was nearly used up at this point). I screeched to a halt on the shoulder, trying to avoid the car coming from the left. I did avoid the car, but I ran out of space and stumbled, tripping myself up and landing on my hands and knees. I quickly saw that I'd gotten away with a few scratches. So I picked myself up and took on the last mile into Wooster with a broad grin on my face, knowing the ride had been worth the fall a hundred times over...

The *Super 8* motel I was planning to stay at was on the way out of the city where there were no restaurants, so I decided to make a short detour through downtown. Adding more distance seemed borderline insane on this epically long day, but I needed some real food. I'm glad I went the extra mile, because Wooster turned out to be a beautiful town with historic buildings and real character:

'Finally some civilization', I thought. I sensed a familiarity, surrounded by warm lights and restaurants and people who were dressed up and out on the town. As I made my way to the Chinese restaurant I had found on Yelp, I felt myself yearning for some time in one of the bars I passed. I wanted the feeling of a cool beer in my hand, and maybe strike up a conversation with a stranger. Or even join a group of people, and we'd all raise our glass and drink to life and friends and good company. Or better yet, to Bernie Sanders. But I couldn't. I needed to get to my motel to rest and ice my legs as soon as possible. After picking up my food I was rewarded with this beautiful view when I crossed a bridge on the final stretch to the *Super 8*:

By the way, I hadn't forgotten about my vow to boycott Super 8 on this trip, after what had happened in Valparaiso. But convenience won a clear victory against integrity on this one.

110

After my daily hot bath I ate my Chinese food and watched TV, reminding myself that I had made it more than halfway through Ohio. Two more days, then I would finally be crossing into Pennsylvania, by far the widest of the states I'd be traveling through - almost half the mileage of the entire trip. 'Stay positive', I told myself. 'One day at a time. You made it this far, you can make it the rest of the way.'

My friend Lisa back in LA called me. We hadn't spoken in a while. 'How's everything? I saw you got engaged. Congrats!' (awkward pause) 'We broke up actually', I said. 'Oh, I'm sorry to hear that. What happened?' she asked. 'Well, you know...' I responded. 'Hard to explain.' We spoke about my walk instead, the overall political situation and my screenplay she had come on board to produce: *a (true) story from 13th century Norway, where two warriors go on a perilous journey across the mountains in the deep of winter to save the late King's secret son - an infant boy* (I'm sure their feet hurt as well).

After we hung up I realized how good it had felt to hear a familiar voice. My bones still ached, but my spirit was revived.

As I went to sleep that night I had no idea how much that spirit would be tested the following day... Of the brutal challenge that lay ahead, and the emotional purgatory it would plunge me into... I just closed my eyes and slipped away into dream land.

Day 13 - planned destination: Canton, OH

I stopped to rest, having reached approximately the halfway point for that day. It had been a quiet journey, but exhausting nonetheless. I always sought out spots with a bit of a climb, so it was easier for me to sit down, and get back up. The break wasn't meant to be more than ten minutes, maximum. But it would turn out to last a lot longer...

I sipped on Gatorade as I grabbed my phone. I was curious to find out about a rally that was going to take place that day, where Bernie Sanders and Hillary Clinton would appear together for the first time. There had been rumors about a possible endorsement of Senator Sanders for the former Secretary during that event, but I didn't believe it for a second. Bernie Sanders knew how to play the game if he had to, sure, but an endorsement was out of the question. After all, he was still an active candidate in this race. But before I was even able to pull up the video of the rally, the posts on my Facebook feed left no doubt: people everywhere expressed their disbelief, and some even disappointment in Bernie. Many said this was it, that Bernie's campaign was dead. My heart beat like a drum, and I could feel the heat of my blood rushing to my face - the sensations of anticipating bad news. I found the clip. I watched it. A part of me still refused to believe it, but it was true: Bernie Sanders had endorsed Hillary Clinton.

Remember the beginning of the book? We're back. This is it. I already shared with you that I felt as defeated and low as I deemed possible at that point. Everything I had gone through had been in vain. My walk was rendered pointless. There was no more reason for me to drag myself through the country. The race was over. My friends told me to get on the next plane, and I felt a deep yearning to go home. To leave this ordeal behind, and cut my losses. I had tried, hadn't I? I had really tried. What more could I do? And then, just as I was about to continue to the next town, to find the quickest way back to Chicago, get my Jeep and drive straight back to Los Angeles to pick up my life where I left off, I noticed the before mentioned mailbox across the street. The rusty one, remember? It took me a moment to put together the letters written on it, but I soon realized that this sign wasn't just literally a sign, it was also a *figurative* one. A message. A wink from the Universe. Or the Divine. Or whatever you want to call it. And it was a message that couldn't have been simpler, or clearer, or more beautiful, or more desperately needed! And I suddenly knew without a smidgen of a doubt that - despite the hopelessness and despair of my situation - I was supposed to be here. Right here in Bumfuck, OH. Far away from home, on some crazy quest I had decided to take on for reasons only the stars knew. And that every experience in my life, absolutely everything and all I had ever done and gone through, had lead me here. And that I wasn't going home after all - not for all the money in the world!

And this what I saw...

BURNI ON.

Of all the possible last names in the United States - there are about 150,000 - the name of whoever lived here was BURNISON. And of the eight letters, the one that was completely faded was the S, leaving: BURNI ON. I don't know about you, but I can only think of one way to pronounce this, and that is:

BERNIE ON!

Can you understand my disbelief now? My awe? For some reason I had sat down to rest exactly across from this house on my 734 mile walk for Bernie Sanders, and right when I was hit with the worst news possible - news specifically in regards to Bernie's campaign, and which seriously made me consider turning around and going home - I looked up and saw those words. Can anyone really argue that this wasn't a sign? Or a pointer, or a message, or whatever the heck you want to call it? Can anyone really hear this - and I swear on everything that is sacred to me that it happened exactly the way I'm telling you it did - and argue that it's a *coincidence*? I can't imagine anyone would.

114

Still unable to grasp what had just happened I set out. I sent the picture to John-Michael and Becca - we had been messaging back and forth after hearing about the endorsement, crying on each other's shoulders - and they couldn't believe what I shared with them. 'You have to post it on your page!' they urged me. I did. And I also shared it on the *Bernie Sanders Activists* page where I'd gotten into the habit of posting status updates and where thousands of people supported me every day with likes, reactions and comments. Some people said they got chills when they saw the picture. There was no way around this being a sign of some sort. And that I should continue, despite the devastating news that day.

I had so much to process. I didn't understand what had happened. How could I? I still racked my brain about the real meaning of it. What was I supposed to take from it? Did this sign mean finishing my walk was important, maybe even beyond the presidential race? I didn't know. Sometimes the most powerful things in life are impossible to explain or understand. They're bigger, or deeper, than our intellect. But being there in that moment - given the circumstances and the shape I was in and seeing what I saw with my own eyes - triggered a decision deep inside me that I can't even say I had any involvement with on a conscious level, and I certainly didn't have the power to unmake it: this walk was now a sacred mission. So, after putting a couple of miles behind me and taking my lunch break outside a gas station, I made another post on Facebook:

This walk isn't over until I put my hands on the f***ing fence they erected around the Wells Fargo Center. End of story.

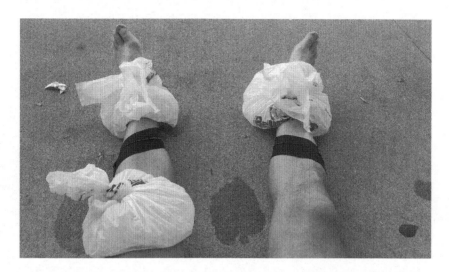

I wanted to show my defiance and my resolve. I wanted to rally Bernie's supporters to not give up on him. It made me feel like a leader, and it gave me strength.

A few people walking in and out of the gas station asked if I was okay. I got curious looks from almost everyone. But I was used to it by that point. I didn't care if they thought I was a trekker, or homeless, or crazy - I just wanted to get to my destination without hurting myself more, or running out of steam.

When I had finished my food and had iced my legs for long enough, I took on the last 10 miles of the day. Unfortunately, the pain and fatigue soon returned. But there was also encouraging news. News that filled me with hope again, looking forward: everywhere on Facebook information popped up about the *real* reason behind Bernie Sanders' endorsement of Hillary Clinton. And - while I wasn't shocked - the degree of corruption and general insanity within the Democratic party and its rules and regulations still managed to surprise me: as the candidate with

116

less pledged delegates Senator Sanders had no choice but to make the endorsement. Had he refused, the party would have been within its rights to withdraw from him his spot at the convention in Philadelphia, and in effect end his campaign. For good. As crazy and infuriating as it was, it was also reassuring. I knew there had to have been more to this story. Bernie Sanders wouldn't just throw everything he had fought for overboard, and join the other side. The system was powerful, and he simply had no choice. As some people accurately put it: he fell on his sword for us. But the most important thing was that he hadn't conceded. He was still an active candidate. And he would still fight for the nomination at the convention in two weeks. I realized that Bernie Sanders was still as much a revolutionary as he had been on any given day throughout his campaign, and now he needed us to read between the lines. He was in a way a political hostage, who had to play by the rules and take a painful hit to still have a shot at winning the war. 'Good', I thought. 'We're still in this.'

I had never been to Indiana, as I said before. But, traveling through, I had seen enough of it to know that it's not exactly a wealthy and flourishing state. It was rough. Broken down in many places. Buildings needed renovating. Public areas had a feeling of decay about them. Massillon, OH, was no different: I walked through this city being particularly aware of this. I couldn't not be. Everything about it seemed edgy. People had a toughness and roughness about them - a hard look in their eyes. It's difficult to explain the feeling you get when coming through a new city, or even crossing into another state, but there's an energy, accumulated from its history and the collective of all the people living there and having lived there. Massillon, OH, had a dangerous touch to its atmosphere. Certainly a rough edge. And so did my destination of Canton, OH, which was only a few more miles down the road. I learned later that I stayed in what is probably the worst part of town, and my experience of the city was limited to that, so take this with a grain of salt. But, wow, I didn't know where I had landed... I had assumed that, since the

Canton Inn - my resting place for the night - had a good official ring to its name, I would find a nice accommodation waiting for me. And even an acceptable one would have done. I was so tired, I didn't really care about comfort. But on the last stretch to the motel I thought I had landed in some communist country, where everything was crumbling and rusting away, and no one feels the need to fix or renovate things. It was ugly:

There was a liquor store across the street from the motel where two guys were dancing and flirting with what were clearly working girls - and not the classy kind. They had their car doors open, blasting some music they were dancing to until the owner came out and told them to beat it. Somebody shuffled across the street in old worn out clothes, looking nervously over their shoulder. Outside the motel a handful of men and women drank out of plastic cups, heavily intoxicated. The stairs leading up to the entrance were cracked open and crumbling... I was still clinging on to the hope that the inside wouldn't match the outside. 'How bad can it be?' I thought.

After I paid $45 (remember that amount - it's the same I would pay later at the most charming motel I've ever been to) for a room on the third floor, I headed up the staircase. I was so spent, all I could think about was how I didn't want to climb stairs right now, but the terrible condition this place was in still distracted me. Now, maybe I just haven't seen a lot of rundown motels in my life, but this was bad: the blueish-green carpet was so old and dirty it was dissolving and breaking up everywhere. The paint on the walls was coming off left and right. Again, I had the feeling of being in some third world country. What was I getting myself into

119

in this dilapidated building, with the questionable guests lingering in and outside, ever on edge and suspicious?

I opened the door to my room. It was pretty gross, I could see that at first glance. The carpet had dark stains that could have been anything from dark liquor or paint, to blood. I accidentally grazed the bed frame with my foot as I walked in, and instantly some part came off. I tried to put it back, but there was nothing holding it in place. The wall paint was ancient, and so was the TV. I put down my things, reminding myself that all I had to do was sleep here. I would simply spend as little time as possible in this motel, and leave at the crack of dawn. Case settled.

That's when I heard the rustling in the wall... Chills ran down my spine. My immediate thought was: rodent. Or a giant roach. The noise came from behind the rusty appliance in the wall that could only have been the AC/heater unit. But - I'm not kidding you - it looked like nothing I'd ever seen before. It was just some unidentifiable rusty metal thing that was way too small to fill the ugly hole in the wall. And so there was plenty of space on either side for whatever was in there to crawl out. I tried to take a closer look but then stopped myself, realizing there was no way I'd stay in this room, no matter what kind of animal it was. I wasn't going to pay $45 to wake up to a rat sharing my bed. I had some pride left, exhausted or not.

I headed back down and told the owner I needed a new room, or a refund. He said there were no refunds and asked what the problem was. I told him the problem, and his only reply was that it couldn't possibly be, after all he had just gotten the AC brand new. I swallowed my comment about the ridiculousness of that statement and told him he had to give me a different room. Finally, he handed me the keys to a room on the first floor, which he would usually charge $60 for, since it had a King bed. I didn't even acknowledge this obvious attempt to make himself look generous, grabbed the key and my things and headed to my new room. 'First floor', I thought. 'Not sure if that's better, considering the folks who are hanging out in the parking lot right outside the window...'

I opened the door to my room, hoping it would be better than the last one. And it was - at least at first glance. I first noticed the hundred or more fruit flies when I opened the curtains and a swarm of them scattered. There were some regular sized flies as well, but only a handful. 'Great', I thought. 'So I'll be sleeping with flies all over me.' For a second I debated with myself, then I decided to just accept it and deal with it. I needed to rest, ice my legs, and - do my laundry. I had run out of clean socks and underwear, and - while I didn't mind wearing a dirty and stained Bernie T-shirt during the day - I was not going to sink low enough to wear my sweaty underwear twice. Nope. The question if this motel had a guest washing machine and dryer popped into my head, but was quickly answered by my own laughter: *sure* it would. I might still have made the effort to ask, but - as I had quickly realized - there were no phones in any of the rooms to call through to the front desk. And since the chances were about one in a million, I wasn't going to take extra steps to walk there and ask in person. Earlier, when I had paid for the room, the owner had given me a styrofoam container for the bag of ice I had bought at the liquor store across the street. I hadn't even asked for it, and I thought that was nice of him. Now it would serve me as washing machine. I had bought a travel portion of Tide at a CVS earlier in the day, and I filled the container with hot water, poured in the Tide and soaked my dirty clothes for about half an hour. I hung everything up to dry, knowing my clothes would most likely still be wet the next morning, but I preferred that to being dirty and smelly. As I got ready for bed my sister Verena messaged me from Austria, asking how things were. I sent her this photo:

I told her this was how I was going to sleep that night, because the motel was disgusting. She laughed, expressed her empathy and wished me the best for the next day. I took a shower and went to bed.

Day 14 - planned destination: Lisbon, OH

The next morning I left the *Canton Inn* as fast I could, though not as early as I had hoped. My body needed more rest than I was able to give. I headed out around 9am, and I sincerely hope I will never be back. Before I tackled the majority of the 35 miles to Lisbon, I stopped at a McDonald's for some breakfast and coffee. I had seen more and more information popping up online about the true reasons behind Bernie's endorsement of Hillary Clinton. In a live stream on my page I shared my thoughts on the situation. I had no doubt that Senator Sanders' hand was forced, and that he needed us to fight on, despite what he was coerced into saying on national TV.

I don't recall much of my travel that day. But as I'm writing this, I can see on Google maps that there's another 20-mile straight between Canton and Lisbon - I guess I blocked that ordeal from my memory.

Lisbon, OH, is a small, but curiously charming town. I remember walking in, feeling a sense of comfort as I looked around. Maybe it was just the perfect summer evening mood as the sun was setting, and the houses were alight with a warm orange color. Again - as I had felt in Wooster before - I longed for company. Sitting over a glass of wine with someone. Making small talk. Or big talk. Or something in between. Just get a dose of civilization. But I decided against getting dinner, and headed straight for the *Traveler's Motel* at the other end of town.

As I entered the motel office I remembered how close I now

was to the Pennsylvania border. The next day, if everything went according to plan, I would be close enough to Pittsburgh to spend the night at my friend Luke's place. The thought filled me with hope.

I was greeted by a friendly Indian couple. Their names were Mahendrabhai and Amitaben Patel. I know, because after I paid for my room and told them about my journey - which they were very curious about - they invited me to have dinner with them. I could tell they were taken with my efforts, and maybe also a little worried about my health and safety. I gladly accepted their offer. Before we ate, however, Mahendrabhai drove me back into town (there was no ice machine at the motel). He was a polite and talkative man, and I enjoyed listening to him in his thick Indian accent. He told me about his children, about where they lived, their occupation, and how often he and his wife travelled to see them. He was very proud of the motel property, and told me of his plans of expanding it. I had already noticed earlier how well he took care of everything, and he sounded like a good business man who valued structure, and planning ahead. 'I can learn a thing or two from him', I caught myself thinking.

I wish I could remember the names of all the Indian dishes Amitaben put on the table after we returned, but let it suffice to say they were delicious. And I felt a warm gratitude in my heart for being invited into the couple's private space - I was a perfect stranger, after all. In our conversation I couldn't help but bring up their last name: Patel. If you're from India or have family there you'll know this, of course, but I had only just recently discovered what a widespread name *Patel* was. Mahendrabhai confirmed all the facts I had learned, and how there were actual conventions in the United States, where parents tried to find the right Patel man or woman for their son or daughter to marry (if you get the chance check out the great documentary 'Meet the Patels', and you'll know what I mean). Before I said good night, Amitaben asked if I would join them for breakfast early next morning before setting out. 'I would be glad to', I said.

I got up to light rain and a gray sky. My room was very comfortable and I felt rested after a good night's sleep, but the roads were wet outside, and I was instantly filled with concern for my journey that day. I had a long way to go if I wanted to make it to the suburbs of Pittsburgh, and scooting on wet asphalt would be dangerous. I sent a silent prayer out into the Universe as I headed to the Patel's room to join them for breakfast. I cannot emphasize enough what human kindness does to lift your spirit, especially when you're going through a tough and challenging time. And sitting there with this lovely couple over Indian breakfast, as Mahendrabhai talked about his plans of adding a little shop to the motel - it was smart business, since there was no convenience store within a couple of miles - chased my worries away:

(Mahendrabhai and Amitaben Patel)

By the time breakfast was over the rain had diminished to a mere drizzle, and soon the roads would be dry: prayer answered. I thanked the Patels for their hospitality and their warm company, and set out.

Day 15 - planned destination: Pittsburgh, PA

I don't know how familiar you are with East Ohio and Pennsylvania, but I was soon reminded of something Ian had made me aware of when we first looked at possible routes for my walk: there would be mountains, no matter which angle I'd be approaching from. I remembered that I had scoffed at the elevation - the highest point would be 3,000 feet, and where I come from that's called a *hill* - but it did look like a lot of ups and downs for a substantial amount of miles, and now I was slowly starting to feel the reality of that.

After going on and off the highway for the first 20 or so miles, I came across a big junction where the 30, the 267 and the Ohio Scenic River Byway form a big knot. I remember this spot because I was caught aback by a fast car (surprise, surprise - it wasn't a pedestrian friendly crossing) and had to fall into a light run to make it across the road. Only in retrospect I realized that I had *run* (it was really a careful jog) for the first time since setting out, and - still increasing the distance I walked each day - this subconscious act instilled new hope in me that I would be able to leave the scooter behind soon.

I crossed through a town called East Liverpool next and it was utterly depressing: the place reminded me of other towns and cities I'd seen before, that seemed to lack so many things human beings need for a healthy standard of living... It was crumbling wherever I looked. A guy I passed on the street just glanced at me with an empty look in his eyes, unable or unwilling to return my chipper *hello*. 'What do you do when you grow up in a place like

126

this?' I thought. People who say everyone can create the future they want for themselves don't understand that what surrounds us when we're children *becomes* us - it's in every fiber of our being. Of course there are exceptions, but most people can't imagine or dream their way out of a place that gives them nothing when they grow up. The options just aren't there.

It was to be expected that the bridge I came upon next was one of the rustiest and derelict structures I have seen:

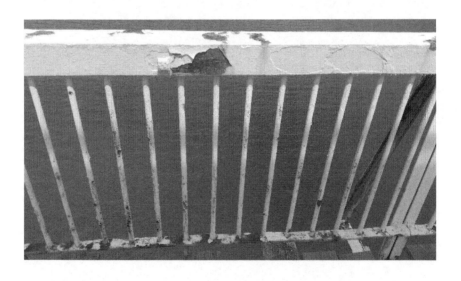

128

I've never been scared crossing a bridge in my life, but I couldn't get off the *Newell Toll Bridge* fast enough. Bernie's words about our crumbling infrastructure - the bridges, the roads, the airports, the rail system, etc. - came to mind. What a perfect example this was... The urgency of the matter aside, isn't it embarrassing that we live in the wealthiest country in the world, and yet things are rusting and falling apart all over? What do they have in Japan, Germany, France, Norway, Sweden, and so many other countries that we don't have? I'll let you answer that question...

As I stepped off on the other side, taking a breath of relief, I was surprised to see this sign:

I had totally overlooked that I would be crossing through a tiny sliver of West Virginia before entering Pennsylvania, but then it wasn't long before it finally happened:

You'll remember what I had decided back in Indiana: if I could make it to Pennsylvania nothing would stop me. And here I was! I tried to message my friend Luke as I was sitting in the shade under the ruins of what once must have been a gas station - and I mean *ruins* - but I had no signal. So I spent the rest of my break looking around this eerie abandoned place, as cars rushed past thirty feet from where I sat... There was something foreboding about my first encounter with Pennsylvania. Maybe I'm making this up, but I really felt like I could sense its energy: it was hard, tough and intimidating. Loud and angry. Of course I would soon be marveling at the beauty this state had to offer - its forests and wildlife are breathtaking - but in that moment I couldn't help but think that Pennsylvania wouldn't go easy on me (in time I would find out how right I was, and that what I had gone through so far was a walk in the park in comparison to what lay ahead. But more of that later...).

Meanwhile, back on the road, I had put a few more miles behind me and was confused as I found myself on an empty gravel road in the midst of trees. 'Did I go the right way?' I thought, as I checked the route on my GPS. I did. 'Am I really going to have to push the scooter across gravel for the next two miles?' And just as I surrendered to my fate and went ahead, cursing every time the wheels got stuck in the gravel, a hiker appeared ahead. He asked where I was going as we passed, curious to know why I was pulling my scooter along this off road. I showed him my route, and explained that I was trying to get to Pittsburgh. 'You're lucky I caught you', he said. 'The bridge at the end of this road is under repair. There's no way across, even for a pedestrian.' He told me there was an easy way around and he would be walking in my direction for a bit. I couldn't believe my luck. The thought alone of going like this for two miles, only to find out that I had to turn around and walk back the same way, was unbearable (next time you've got a scooter at hand try to roll it over a stretch of gravel: you'll soon curse the day you were born, trust me).

So, Ted - that was the Gentleman's name - and I headed uphill together, through a quiet and peaceful area, where there were only a few properties nestled in the trees here and there. Ted told me he was 73, had two heart surgeries behind him, and now went for long walks four times a week to stay healthy. I told him a bit about my quest, and soon we had reached the point where our paths would separate again:

(Ted)

Ted said something very nice before he shook my hand goodbye: 'We've only just met, but talking with you I feel like I've known you for a long time.' He waved as he went up the hill. I waved back, stepped on the scooter and let it roll down the other side. The rough road hurt my wrists, however, and I soon stopped and walked the rest of the decline.

The suburbs of Pittsburgh are where I first took notice of the jungle-like forests of Pennsylvania. It had rained recently and the roads were still wet. I remember having to very carefully head down a steep hill so as to not slip and fall, but all I wanted to do was stare at the incredibly lush and dense emerald forests around me. I felt like I had landed on the Jurassic Park island, there was such beauty and wildness to them.

Luke had agreed to pick me up close to the *Neville Island Bridge* in Moon, PA, about 15 miles outside of central Pittsburgh. I was early and used the time to capture the dramatic sunset this evening:

It was still warm out and I enjoyed the summer night atmosphere, despite being exhausted beyond belief. Behind where I sat was an old church, and on its lawn fireflies started to show as daylight was quickly fading. A lone bird sat on the grass, and I realized that he was waiting for the fireflies to light up, so he could make his move and catch them. It was highly entertaining: the fireflies clearly had their fun with the poor bird, who ran around erratically, changing direction at every flash of light, and never even getting close to catching one of them.

Just after 9pm Luke's car pulled up. He jumped out, grinning ear to ear and gave me a big hug. It was so comforting to see one of my best friends after being out on my own for over two weeks at this point. We loaded the scooter and backpack in the trunk and drove off.

The half hour drive to the apartment suite Luke's family was staying at was too short to properly catch up. Luke wanted to know everything about my journey, and I had many questions regarding the reason he and his family were currently in Pittsburgh: his father Fred had undergone a very serious surgery and I knew that the last months had been testing for Luke, to say the least (the surgery went well, and Fred is on a good path of recovery).

We arrived. Luke's mom Joan and his brother Kent welcomed me, and I thanked them for letting a smelly and sweaty trekker like me stay the night. I took a long hot shower and then they fed me and did my laundry for me, knowing I was too exhausted to spend any more energy that night:

(Kent and Luke Moran)

I was grateful, but not surprised - the Morans had always treated me like family. As much as I enjoyed my friends' company, I had a hard time relaxing. I began to feel myself enveloped by the homely atmosphere, and I could sense something inside me resisting. I was afraid that if I didn't stay in the mind set I needed to be in - namely focused, tough and resilient - I wouldn't be able to finish my walk. Another matter kept bouncing around in my head: I had been playing with the idea to leave the scooter behind for a few days now, and - considering that I would still be in the vicinity after my next stop - this seemed like the perfect opportunity. So the next morning, after Luke drove me back to the spot he had picked me up the night before, I left the scooter with him.

Day 16 - planned destination: North Versailles, PA

I planned to walk 15 miles into Pittsburgh where I would meet Luke for lunch, and then reassess if I should leave the scooter behind for good. And with the security of knowing I could still get it back if I had to, I set out.

I felt vulnerable. Naked. I know it sounds strange, but I had gotten so used to having my hands on the scooter handles - either rolling along or pushing it - that now it felt like something was missing. I wondered how my body would hold up without this crutch. The prior day I had walked somewhere between 10 and 15 miles and my feet had been doing fine. But that was a mile or so at a time, before I would hop on the scooter again. Today I'd be walking straight for at least 15 miles.

I made sure that I properly rested my feet during every break. I even massaged them, and I did the same for my calves. And after finishing 8 miles in just over two hours I allowed myself some optimism: this didn't feel too bad.

Crossing a bridge into downtown Pittsburgh, I got a nice view of *Heinz Stadium*:

This was my first time visiting Pennsylvania's second largest city. The prior night, from the passenger seat of Luke's car, I hadn't gotten to see much of it, but now I was walking straight through its center in bright daylight. It was a curious feeling: downtown Pittsburgh reminded me of New York City, where I had lived for two and a half years after moving to the US. Back then I was just like the young, driven workaholics hurrying along the sidewalk. Now, almost a decade later, I was a whole different person on a whole different journey...

I passed some beautiful and historic architecture (I think much of it was University buildings) and soon I was only a mile or two away from Luke's apartment. And that's where it hit me again: the curse of the final stretch. It was hot out that day and I had walked fast, maybe too fast for what was essentially a tryout distance. And now I could feel every step in my muscles and bones. The final mile seemed to extend into eternity. 'How is my backpack this heavy?' I thought, doing my best not to fall into despair. Then, after what felt like a never-ending struggle, Luke's voice called out from across the street: I had finally made it. I was on the wrong side of the street, though, and had walked past the entrance. God, how I was looking forward to breaking for lunch!

Once inside, I put up my legs and wrapped my knees and feet in ice packs, while eating pizza and drinking delicious organic grapefruit juice. I was tired, and my mind wasn't ready to accept the fact that I had to get up and do more of the same very soon. But I strictly wanted to stick to a 30-minute break. I had between 11 and 13 miles left to go, depending on which route I would take and what motel I would stay at, and I didn't want to walk deep into the night. Luke said he wanted to accompany me for a couple of hours, and he didn't mind bringing the scooter along, which would give me another short window to decide if I was going to leave it behind or not.

And so we walked, a second body next to mine for the first time on my journey. It was great to have my friend along, but it was also frustrating to see him stroll along with such ease. I felt weak and fragile in comparison and the truth is, I was, of course.

We passed through some poor and rundown neighborhoods before heading up a steep hill. We were definitely leaving central Pittsburgh now and Luke decided this was a good spot for him to stop, to still be able to get an Uber. He asked if I wanted to leave the scooter with him, and I finally had to decide: if I left it I wouldn't be able to get it back. And where I was heading I couldn't get another one that easily, not to mention that I didn't have another $200 to spend on a second scooter. I was torn. 'I'll go on without it. I think my feet will hold up', I finally told him as the Uber arrived. I thanked Luke and we hugged goodbye. I knew I would see him soon (he's a filmmaker in LA, just like myself). He wished me all the best and told me to keep him posted. I promised I would, and moments later I watched him drive away - with my scooter. You've probably seen the movie 'Cast Away'? If you haven't, here's a quick synopsis: *'After a plane crash a Fed Ex employee is stranded on a remote island, where a volley ball he names Wilson becomes his only companion. After four years of waiting for rescue the man leaves the island on a makeshift boat. At sea a storm hits and Wilson floats away. The man can't recover the ball, and mourns it like a lost friend.'*

I know my own situation wasn't quite as dramatic, but I did have a bit of a Wilson moment watching my scooter drive off. The feeling of being vulnerable and naked returned - and this time it was for good. It was nothing but me and my legs now, and the last time I had set out like this I hadn't gotten very far:

'You've grown stronger', I reassured myself. 'It took some time to get used to, but now your body will be able to deal with it. Have faith.' And so I set my route on Google Maps, called ahead to a *Super 8* motel about 7 miles away to reserve a room, and headed out.

And everything went pretty well, until three hours in and after ascending a brutally steep and seemingly never-ending hill in almost complete darkness, I realized I had gone the wrong way... It only dawned on me when I thought myself fairly close - 2 miles or so - to the *Super 8*. I checked my phone to see the exact distance left, and realized in horror that I had followed a completely different path (earlier I had debated between two different routes, and then clearly set the wrong one on my GPS). So now I was nowhere near the *Super 8*, the landscape turned more and more rural, and I had no idea if there were any possible accommodations in the area at all! Add to that my fatigue and the time being after 10pm already, and you can imagine the worry creeping up on me: this wasn't a good start. I checked for motels on my phone. I couldn't see anything on the path ahead at first, and when I finally found something, it was another two hours away and I couldn't reach the owner when I called. The last thing I needed was to walk the distance and then, after midnight and in the middle of nowhere, realize the motel wasn't in business anymore. But I didn't really have a choice. I had to trust the place still existed and that they'd have a room available.

I went ahead on the dark road, the last strength for the day leaving my body at faster and faster rate. Just before 11pm I saw some lights ahead. There was a Dunkin' Donuts still open. I willed myself to make the 0.3 miles there, so I could eat something and rest a bit before heading on. It was like entering a glamorous 5 star restaurant: there were still plenty of people out and about, laughing and talking. Music played, and everyone seemed at ease as they ordered their favorite donut or drink. I put down my things and sat by a table. I looked around, wanting nothing more than to talk to someone. To make a human connection. I felt so out of place. Disconnected from civilization.

A nomad...

I tried again to call the motel I had found earlier, but again no one picked up. Desperate thoughts formed in my mind: 'Could I ask any of these people for shelter, in case I don't find an accommodation? Really, where will I sleep if this falls through? Please let it work out somehow...', I begged the Universe. After I finished my sandwich and orange juice, I decided to leave this lively and colorful oasis behind, and head out. My knees were so incredibly stiff, I could barely lift my legs off the ground. The next mile and a half would be brutal, there was no doubt about that.

And then something wonderful happened: right across the hill, maybe 0.2 miles from the Dunkin' Donuts, a motel appeared like out of a dream. The *Siesta Motel* hadn't shown up on my search before - why, I don't know. It was open. But it was small, and I prayed they had vacancies as I headed for the office. I didn't know the man behind the counter from Adam, but he instantly became my favorite human when he confirmed they had rooms available. My inner self was jumping up and down with joy and relief, and then momentarily stopped when I heard the words: 'No cards. Cash only.' I didn't have enough cash on me. I tried my best persuasion tactics, and asked more than once if there was any way we could do this, so I didn't have to walk back down to the gas station to squeeze real money out of the ATM. But my favorite human simply shook his head *no*. 'Alright', I thought. 'At least I've got a room. I can do another 0.5-0.6 miles. Or can I...?' I asked if I could leave my stuff in the office until I was back, and the man begrudgingly agreed.

I went outside. In the parking lot a man and a woman who had just decided to find a different motel were about to get into their car. I was so worried about walking even ten more steps that night, I was a breath away from asking them if I could get a ride. But then I decided against it. It was late and dark. I was dirty and smelly. I didn't want to put them in an uncomfortable position. So - without the scooter to help me in situations like these - I walked back down the hill. Just like two weeks earlier in Valparaiso, IN, the concept of walking back the way I came was completely ludicrous to me. Every step seemed to mock my tired and aching body. But - after meeting the nicest gas station employee in probably all of Pennsylvania - I was soon back with the required amount of bills, and a bag of ice.

Exiting the office, I found a young guy and a basically unconscious girl on the bench outside. I asked what had happened and he told me she had blacked out from drinking. He had come to pick her up, but she was almost entirely unresponsive. I offered some of the ice to maybe hold to her neck or something, and he gladly accepted. There were voices in my head saying this or that could *really* be going on, but it's hard to assess a situation like this without knowing more. The young man seemed sincere so I left them to it, hoping they really were friends and the girl would recover quickly so he could bring her home. I had to take care of myself now, though I remember thinking I'd rather be in the state I was in, than poisoned by that much alcohol.

Taking a hot bath on that night was nothing short of glorious. I was so grateful for my room, and I felt reasonably optimistic. I had made it through my first day without the scooter - it was possible! On top of that a woman named Jessica, who lived in the area, had reached out on Facebook, offering to provide breakfast the next morning. I gladly accepted, looking forward to spending some time with another Bernie supporter, and we agreed to meet at the Dunkin' Donuts at 9am the next day.

I wanted to take good care of my body that night and so I iced my feet and knees for an entire episode of 'Person of Interest', popped one magnesium and one glucosamine pill (I had gotten them at some pharmacy a few days prior) for my bones and joints, and then rubbed Arnica gel on my muscles before tucking myself in. I let my weight sink into the sheets, consciously feeling through my body from head to toe, and asking it to take over and do its healing work while I was sleeping. The following day would give me a better understanding of the shape I was in...

Day 17 - planned destination: Ligonier, PA

I felt good when I got up. Not good enough to not care about walking back some of the distance *again*, but hey. And - free breakfast aside - it would soon turn out that meeting Jessica was well worth the sacrifice.

I could make her out from afar as I was once again heading for the Dunkin' Donuts. She had a Bernie T-shirt on and her two little kids with her: her daughter Cadence and her son Preston. We smiled, said hello, and hugged. Again, there was not much ice to break. There was an unspoken understanding, that if someone was rooting for Bernie, they were rooting and caring for everyone else in this country and on this planet, and that was enough to trust them wholeheartedly.

A few minutes later we were already munching on breakfast sandwiches, while learning a little about each other. Jessica, who - similar to myself - had started out not knowing anything about Bernie Sanders at all, had quickly let her full on support for his campaign consume her life, so to speak. She completely and fully got it. Her eyes were clear and awake, as she gave me an impassioned speech about why we needed this man to lead the country, and needed him badly. Our conversation lifted my spirits and I think Cadence and Preston had a good time, as well. They were such beautiful children. I loved watching them listen to us with big eyes, wondering if they needed to be shy around me or not:

(Jessica with Cadence & Preston)

I didn't have much time to spare, unfortunately, and so we soon had to say goodbye. There was a generosity and openness about Jessica that warmed my heart and made it difficult to part - once again. But she assured me that she would come to Philadelphia to protest, and maybe we would see each other there (which we did). And with that we parted ways.

Like the daily and increasing support on Facebook, encounters like this one carried me forward, there's not a doubt in my mind. And maybe, had Jessica, Cadence and Preston not met with me that morning, I would have never made it through the punishment that lay ahead...

I was very aware that the 26 or 27 miles I had walked the day prior were substantially lower than my average, and that worried me. I needed to put at the very least 32 miles behind me that day. Ideally, 36. Sounds like a lot? It is. One advantage of the scooter had been that I could catch up on mileage when the roads were good. Now, however, I was limited to the engine nature had provided me with - my legs - and could only make somewhere between 3 and 3.5mph. That was it. There were no wheels to carry my forward at 4.5 or 5mph when I needed it. If you do the math, you'll quickly see that with a minimum of 2 hours for breaks there wasn't much time left in the day while walking 30+ miles. And there was another, potentially much bigger issue: the old no-motel-where-I-needed-one problem. There were several accommodations in Greensburg about 17 miles out, which was too short a distance and therefore out of the question. The next motel that showed up on my path was 45 miles away in Jennersburg. Unreachable, even with fresh legs. There was a *Ramada Hotel* in Ligonier, 35 miles away, where a room was $140 a night. I'd have to bite the bullet. Unless my friends back home found a different option that I couldn't see at the moment, there was just no other way. 'Let me call ahead, just in case', I thought. Well, it turned out I wouldn't have to spend all that money on a room at the *Ramada,* because the *Ramada* was completely booked out. And the lady on the phone told me with regret in her voice, that the same would be true for every other place in the area. There was a convention going on or something like that. So even if my friends found some secret accommodation somewhere, chances were there wouldn't be any vacancies. Perfect. This day was already promising to be one helluva good time (insert sarcasm emoji here). I saw no choice but to go on and to hope that something would work itself out. This entire journey was mostly improvised, so what did I expect but to be hit by one challenge after the next?

The sun had not yet fully set when I was already pleading for the day to be over, and instead got surprised with something I hadn't seen much of since driving through Missouri: rain. Dave Damato's orange plastic poncho would finally get its chance to shine. I quickly hid under some overhanging trees as more and more water came down, dug through my backpack, and pulled out the poncho. I shouldered the backpack first - it held all the electronics - and then slipped into the poncho, which easily fit the hunch. And, now waterproof, I carried on.

Maybe it was the hassle of dealing with the rain, or maybe I just didn't take it into account altogether, but soon after this I made a mistake - a mistake that would make the last hours of this day even more unbearable than they would have been already...

Let me explain: the 30 split at some point. Meaning two lanes continued in the direction I was walking in, while the lanes for oncoming traffic separated and made a slight curve, running more or less parallel for several miles, but with hundreds of feet of forest between them. My mistake, to be clear, was that I kept walking *with* traffic. I should have crossed the highway and continued on *against* traffic. The difference really only becomes clear at night.

Now it was still somewhat light out - however darkened by the rain clouds – and my head, torso and equipment were safely covered. The temperature was pretty comfortable, and I wasn't worried about getting too cold. But it would get dark soon, and I only now realized how little moon light the high trees on both sides let through. This wasn't one of those stretches with street lamps or wide open fields - I was walking through dense forest.

A bit later the rain had reduced to a harmless drizzle and it was now so dark that I had to put on my headlamp. And here is where my mistake from earlier turned into a serious safety issue: cars were coming from behind, going up to 70mph on a wet road. I had tried walking on both shoulders (they were less than 3 feet wide) and decided that the left one was safer. If I had been walking against traffic, cars and trucks would have been visible to me ahead of time, and the drivers would have had a better chance to see me, as well. As it was, I had to adjust my headlamp so it was on the side of my head, hoping it would provide enough of a warning. But not every driver has their eyes on the road at all times, and that could make the difference between me living or dying that night... I'm not being dramatic, by the way. Many will tell you that walking on a highway shoulder all day isn't exactly the safest thing to do. For me personally that wasn't a concern. It just didn't scare me. Except, *now* it did.

Thanks to my Guardian Angels I didn't get hit. At one point a pick up truck sped past me so fast and at such close range, that I momentarily froze in place. It didn't help that the driver blasted his/her horn at me. Even without sensitive hearing that would have been a shock. And with the fragile state I was in, this incident almost made me crumble on the side of the road. The reason for feeling particularly weak and fragile? Well, for one, there's a big difference between walking 27 miles and 30+ miles. And the difference only becomes apparent around mile 29 or 30 - but then it hits you like a sledgehammer. I was so spent, I had slowed to a snail pace and didn't know how I was possibly going to make it to Ligonier, where - and this was my absolutely sincere, last-resort plan - I was going to ask the staff at the *Ramada* if they would let me sleep in some storage room or bathroom or something like that. Just somewhere the ground wasn't wet. The second issue were me feet, or the skin on my feet: at first I hadn't minded the sloshy feeling in my shoes, but now I could feel one blister after another forming on every friction point from heel to toes.

I refused to believe I still had more than 3 miles to go in this shape. My body had nothing left to give. My mind was feeding me every doubt and fear it could think up. The wet, dark night seemed primal and intimidating, for all I knew I had no place to sleep for the night, and my toes and heels rubbed painfully at every step - especially when I tried to increase my pace to get this ordeal behind me. In short: it was absolute misery.

In the midst of all this I was given a glimpse of breathtaking beauty. Again, pictures can't really give it justice, but I think you can imagine how wonderful this image appeared looking out from the dark forest:

This night, more than any other on this journey, the uncompromising nature of distance and time made itself known. A mile is a mile, and an hour is an hour - there are no exceptions. As desperately as I hoped some magical circumstance would speed up time or shorten the way, that didn't happen. I had to walk it all, and fast enough to not start out too late the following day, where another 30+ miles were waiting for me. 'Are you f***ing crazy?' I questioned myself. 'What the Hell are you doing?' Then Rodrigo called and told me he had found a 'House with rooms' in Ligonier, very close to the *Ramada*. He said to give the owner a call to let them know when I would be arriving. The room was already paid for. I was so incredibly grateful, words can't describe it. 'How much is it?' I asked him. 'Don't worry about it man', he told me. 'I took care of it.' I knew then that it was expensive. But also that I had the kind of friends, who - despite not having a lot of money and swimming in debt themselves - spontaneously put down $175, so I would have a bed for the night on this crazy trip I decided to take on.

I reached the last mile before I would finally exit the highway, and from there it was going to be just a little more than 0.7 miles to my destination. I will spare you the repetitive scenario of how this last mile on the 30 *did not* want to end. Only this much: I was sincerely starting to question if my Google maps app was malfunctioning. There was no way I had walked less than 0.2 miles since I last checked?!

I reached Ligonier. A tiny, but - from the looks of it - wealthy town. Lots of nice properties lined the road. By the time I arrived at the *Thistledown at Seger House* it was after 11pm and I had 35 miles in my legs. I wish it would have felt like an achievement, but all I could think about was a hot bath, ice and sleep. Lifting my stiff legs up any stairs was a near impossibility at this point, so finding out my room was on the third floor came as a shock. But then I shrugged if off like a boss, because they had an elevator. 'If only I could bend my knees half as far as Hillary Clinton bends the truth', I thought. 'I'd be running up the stairs like a teenage Olympian.'

I got to my room. Any accommodation would have done that night - the thought of lying down on a mattress with soft sheets enveloping my body was poetry in my mind - but this was like a tiny version of a royal suite at a four star hotel (I hope the pictures give you an idea):

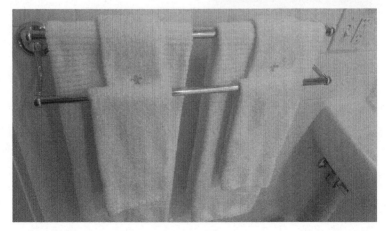

The dichotomy between this preciously decorated, shiny room and my own sweat, dirt and smell, wasn't lost on me. It felt wrong somehow to be in here. I hardly dared touch anything. I sent the pictures to Rodrigo. He deserved to at least see where his money went. One thing I noticed right away, however, was the missing bath tub. I had put all my hopes on soaking my aching body in hot water and epsom salts, to have any chance of continuing on the next day. But a shower would have to do. I asked the owner for a bucket, so I could at least soak my feet. It wasn't perfect, but better than nothing. The simple act of carrying the full bucket of water from the bathroom to the chair right outside was a challenge. I could hardly walk as it was, not to mention carry something this heavy. I sat down and crammed in my feet. The water turned cold quickly, and I knew I didn't have time to fill it up again. I still had to ice my legs and I desperately needed to sleep. If I didn't set out by 9am the next day at the latest, I would have no chance to make it to the next resting place.

I cannot remember ever being this spent and depleted in my entire life. I dragged myself to the bed. Even putting ice on my knees and feet was an ordeal. When I had finally positioned myself, I used the time to record a short video. Really, I didn't feel like lifting a finger, but I wanted to document my journey and I knew this was a special moment. The dark kind, but still special. I was completely raw. I told the camera that this was the hardest thing I had ever done. That I didn't know how to take another step the next day. That keeping going seemed impossible right now.

After 15 minutes I removed the ice, slipped under the covers and whispered to whoever was listening that I needed help. I needed strength for the next day, and for my blisters to heal enough so I could walk... 'Please, please help me.'

Seven and a half hours later I woke up. I felt as stiff as C-3PO, but I saw a tiny sliver of hope. Maybe there was a way forward. I didn't have the courage to put on my shoes yet, so I shuffled to breakfast in my socks. I wore my windbreaker, because I didn't want to expose the other guests to my ragged-looking, smelly

Bernie shirt.

After an egg sandwich and a lovely cup of coffee, I went back to my room. I had no more than four or five band aids left and so I only taped up the blisters I thought would be the most painful ones. Then I grabbed my shoes, took a deep breath and slipped inside. You know when something feels completely and utterly wrong, but for some reason you have to do it anyway? My feet felt like they were on fire from heel to toe, and I was wearing toddler-sized shoes. And now I had to leave on a 30+ mile walk... I cannot begin to tell you how wrong that felt. But here I went - against all reason.

Day 18 - planned destination: Schellsburg, PA

On my way out of Ligonier I passed a pharmacy. I needed more band aids - the good ones - and this could be my saving grace. But it was Sunday, and the pharmacy was closed. Figures. A Dollar General store had to do instead. They didn't have what I needed, so I had no choice but to load up on generic cut-your-finger band aids. Outside, I asked a UPS driver if I could sit on the step at the back of his truck for a minute - it was the only place in the shade. 'No problem', he said. I thanked him and went about taping up my blisters with as many bandaids as I could, while still fitting into the shoes. It wasn't much of a relief, but it was something.

The day ahead looked simple enough logistically: I wouldn't be leaving the 30 once. And I was really getting into rural Pennsylvania now, as the next motel was 38 miles away in a small place called Schellsburg. I didn't delude myself into thinking I could walk 38 miles that day. Not for a single moment. Not after what I had put myself through the day prior. But there was no place else. So I called ahead, and a friendly voice belonging to a man named Bill confirmed that I had my room booked for the night at the *Shawnee Motel*. Now I only needed to get there. I thought to myself that if I had no other choice, I could always hitchhike and get a ride for however much of the distance I couldn't walk (I'll tell you more about that great idea later).

In the present moment I was starting my day, heading down the shoulder of the 30, somewhere between curious and nervous to find out how all of this would go down today. I observed my pace. My inner state. Overall, I felt much better. Sleep does wonders. Darkness fades. Sunlight soothes. The world turns from a menace to a friend... It was a beautiful day out, and the air was clear and fresh as the rain had washed it clean the night before. I had my will and determination back. But how would I manage the pain? Was it possible to repeat what I had done the day before - walk over 30 miles - with a bunch of blisters mixed in? Not to mention the days following? I had no idea.

When you have to walk on a busy highway there's little chance of finding anything but concrete to walk on. And it makes a big difference to have some grass or gravel or mud under your soles every now and then. On the other hand, the paved road is usually very even and you don't have to worry about twisting your ankle, or some piece of gravel putting pressure on a large blister on the side of your heel, resulting in screams of agony and fury. Well, that day it was mostly concrete. Hard, uncompromising concrete.

I remember clearly a stretch somewhere along the way before the sun reached its zenith... I remember it, because at no other time along this walk was my will being tested like it was then and there: I was suffering. There was lots of traffic. It was loud and hot. I looked to the sky, seeing my day wasn't even half done. Then my attention immediately went back to the pulsating pain in my toes and heels. 'This is unbearable', I thought. 'I'm literally torturing myself. How am I going to do another 25,000 steps today, when each single one hurts so much I would refuse to take even one more under normal circumstances?' I knew somehow I had to make it bearable to be able to continue on. I'm not sure how I did it. I think the simplest explanation would be I just didn't stop walking. I know keeping track of my mind helped: any thoughts about how many miles I still had ahead of me, how long it would take until nightfall, how far it still was to Philadelphia, if I was really doing anyone a service with this walk, etc - I had to instantly kill them. Had I not, I would have stopped right there and never continued. Instead, I forced myself to think about two things only: 'The next step. Stay with the next step', I drilled myself. 'Each step brings you closer. Stay present. Next step, next step, next step.' And: 'At some point this will be over. No matter how hard it is right now, at some point the sun will set. All days in the history of planet Earth have ended. There's no exception. This one will, too.' I kept my focus trained on these simple facts, trying to make myself fall into a sort of trance. I fixed my attention on the monotonous rhythm of my legs to hypnotize myself. I wanted to escape into a dreamlike state, so I didn't have to feel the throbbing pain. It helped a bit, as it lent a somewhat surreal feeling to everything for a while. But that ended abruptly when I reached the top of a hill after a long incline, and saw what lay ahead of me... And reality came back with a vengeance:

There's nothing quite like a 4-mile stretch of ups and downs laid out in front of you, in the hottest hours of the day, to make your shoulders drop in defeat. The hills were a normality at this point, and that wouldn't change until I was close to Philadelphia. Walking uphill required muscle work and stamina and depleted my energy faster, but going downhill was worse. It put a lot of pressure on my toes, especially the little ones, which had developed some of the most painful blisters. On top of that, my knee and ankle joints had to support most of my weight. And while the stress fracture in my right foot was healing pretty well from what I could tell, there were other areas - especially in the ball of my large left toe - that were stinging and pinching frequently, and I had no idea what to make of it. 'Who knows what it looks like inside there?' I thought.

I was halfway across that stretch when I got worried about my supply of liquids. I had just drank the last water in my hydration pack and I had half a bottle of Gatorade left. The temperature was somewhere in the mid or high 80s in the shade, and I was sweating so much I hardly had to relieve myself that day. Google maps told me there would be some convenience store coming up a mile and a half or so ahead, but that seemed mightily far. And who knew how up to date the app was in rural areas like these? How could I be sure that store was still in business? I passed a property with several cars parked outside. It looked like they were having a BBQ. For a second I considered asking for water, but then decided against it. Maybe the confederate flags on a couple of the cars had something to do with it...

By the way - I don't know if you know this - but the confederate flag is a common sight in rural Pennsylvania. It is displayed with pride on many lawns, cars, motorcycles, hanging off roofs - you name it. Someone told me that the state technically belongs to the South, so maybe that explains it. But I think you'll agree that - while there's heated debates about what the flag actually stands for based on its history (it is not the 'original confederate flag') – it certainly doesn't celebrate diversity.

I headed on, hoping that this store existed, and was rewarded. After the next elevation a Dollar General materialized on the right side of the road: water and Gatorade to fill buckets with! Phew.

As I beelined for the store I passed a boy on a skateboard. 'Hi', I said. 'Nice day for skating, huh?' He smiled, and greeted back in an open and friendly manner. It surprised me. Kids that age were usually more reserved toward strangers, especially around these areas. This wasn't West Hollywood, where everyone carried their emotions on their sleeve and freely shared personal stories with someone they just met. There was something different about this kid. He had an earnestness about him that made him appear older. All of this went through my head in a mere few seconds as I headed for the entrance.

A few minutes later I sat outside the store, cooling my body in the shade, ice on my knees and feet. I had stocked up on water and Gatorade, and bought some ham, cheese and crackers for lunch. Not exactly ideal nutrition, but it would have to do. As I was struggling to stay focused on resting and recovering, versus worrying about the fact that I still had two thirds of the way ahead of me that day, the boy from before approached me. He seemed to have little inhibitions as he squatted down close by, curiously studying me. 'What is the ice for?' he asked. I told him that my knees and shins hurt from walking far (I found out later from Michael Gibino - the delegate running for Bernie, I mentioned earlier in the book - that you should only ice at night, not during activity. Your muscles get cold and are more susceptible to injury. But I don't think it caused more damage for me, luckily, and it did reduce the pain). The boy - his name was Lukas - took it in. He asked where I was walking to, and I explained to him my quest. He seemed intrigued. He told me he knew of Bernie Sanders and that he really liked him. He would vote for him if he could. Lukas' family had come to the States from Mexico, and he felt that Senator Sanders cared about people like him. I couldn't agree more. He went on to tell me he had several siblings and that life wasn't easy for his family. His sister would have to undergo a heart surgery soon, and it was clear to see how much he loved her and how the possibility of losing her scared him. Lukas' openness and compassion moved me. I could tell that he related not only to his sister, but also to me and others. He was very aware for his age:

(Lukas)

Then it came time to say good bye. The urgency of the 20+ miles I had yet to put behind me made itself known in the back of my mind. I thanked Lukas for providing me with company, and for sharing what he shared. We hugged goodbye. He joined his mother who had just come back from shopping, and I wandered East again.

It was getting into the late afternoon now, and the sun was only a few hours from setting. I had kept pushing forward, knowing I needed to hit at least 30 miles that day. It was excruciating, but somehow I was still on my feet.

Maybe it was the peaceful mood and the air cooling down to perfect temperature. The stillness... All I know is around that time my mind was momentarily flooded with thoughts of people struggling, both in this country and around the world, and my heart filled with an overwhelming feeling of empathy. How many lived in poverty? How many veterans had to sleep on the streets? How many fought with mental illness day in, day out? How many had their homes destroyed by bombs, losing family members or their arms or legs? And suddenly, despite the fatigue and the burning pain in my feet, I felt such intense gratitude wash over me for having two healthy legs to walk on, a healthy body and mind, family and friends who loved me, a roof over my head, that I burst into tears. The tragedy of knowing that somewhere others were suffering at any given time, juxtaposed with my own blessings, was overwhelming. My pain seemed secondary, and it made walking much easier for a bit...

At approximately 27 miles in, I stopped at a gas station for energy bars, a banana and more Gatorade. I was exhausted. Part of me had doubted I was going to make it this far that day. The sun was setting now, and I had less than an hour light left. One thing was certain, I would not reach the *Shawnee Motel* on foot. So I simply decided to keep walking until dark, and then hope for a ride the rest of the way.

After another two miles I again witnessed some of the most breathtaking views just before nightfall:

It was as if the sun wanted to give me a little gift on the way, something to remember and hold on to for the cold and dark of night. 'I will be back soon', she seemed to say. 'Keep me in mind.' Unfortunately, darkness has just as convincing a voice. And it reminds you quite bluntly that you're not safe; that without light and proper sight you're just a weak and helpless creature, stumbling across a narrow paved road drawn straight through the wilderness...

After almost reaching the 30-mile marker I decided that I should give myself a break for the night, and that it was time to execute my brilliant plan: hitchhiking. I'm chuckling to myself as I'm writing this. You can probably guess what happened when I - a male, bearded, 37-year-old trekker - tried to get a ride in the middle of rural Pennsylvania after daylight, by waving my thumb at the passing cars... Exactly. The only reaction I got was one car actually honking at me as they put the pedal to the metal, appalled at the mere attempt of me trying to hitch a ride. After 20 or 30 cars I gave up. I could see the pattern evolving. In hindsight, trying to look harmless by putting on a friendly smile probably increased my creep factor by several degrees. 'Alright then', I thought. 'Last resort. I have to put all my hopes on Bill, the owner of the *Shawnee Motel*.' The faint chance of this man, who I only knew from a two minute conversation on the phone, leaving the office at 9:30pm to get into his car and pick up a complete stranger 8 miles down the road, was literally the only thing keeping me from walking another 3 or 4 hours into the night. Which was not only borderline impossible, but would almost certainly have caused more injuries, and even more likely rendered me unable to move the next day, which could have meant I wouldn't be able to reach Philadelphia in time. Or not at all. I think I only now fully understand what a long shot it was. And I can tell you with near certainty that none of the other 20+ motel owners I encountered would have even thought twice about doing something like this...

But Bill did. I placed the call, unsure how to plead my case. It was a ridiculous request. How could this man take me seriously when I had put myself in this desperate situation? He picked up. I quickly told him I was the trekker who had reserved a room earlier, and if there was any way he or someone he worked with would be able to pick me up 8 miles West on the 30? I had walked all day and it was dark, and I had little strength left. I had a little bit of cash to pay for the gas. 'No problem', he said. 'I'll be there in 15 to 20 minutes. I drive a blue pick up truck. Look for me.' I couldn't believe my ears and just stuttered a dozen *thank yous* before I hung up. I kept walking, revived by the thought that I would be at the motel soon. And sure enough, 20 minutes later a blue pick up drove past, made a U-turn and stopped on the shoulder next to me.

I opened the passenger door and saw Bill's face for the first time: he looked like an angel to me. I laughed with the most heartfelt joy and told him that he was my new hero. He smiled, and said it was not a problem at all, and that I looked like I needed to rest. I confirmed his observation as I quickly produced the $17 of cash I had on me, and handed it to him. 'No', he said. 'I don't need any money.' I tried to persuade him. 'It will make me feel better', I told him. 'You don't understand how much you're helping me.' He laughed and told me to keep my money. It was not a big thing at all.

I'm choking up as I'm writing this. God, was I lucky. The unconditional kindness this man showed me in a moment when I was completely at his mercy, moves me in the deepest depths of my heart:

(Bill)

As we came into Schellsburg, Bill pointed to a house on the right of the road, and told me he grew up there. He now lived at the motel property a little further down the road, but Schellsburg had been his home all his life. I quietly scolded myself. I had seen so many Trump signs and confederate flags in Pennsylvania, and - as I mentioned earlier - the state had a rough and tough energy to it, that I had subconsciously labeled its people as the same. To learn that someone who had lived in a small town like this their entire life, and yet be so open to a stranger, was surprising. And humbling.

We reached the *Shawnee Motel*. It was pretty. Unlike other motels, the architecture was appealing and it looked like it had history. Bill told me that it had been run by his wife Thelma's side of the family since the 50s, and he and Thelma had taken over a couple of decades ago. When we entered the office - just like the outside everything in here had a charming character - Thelma, Bill's wife, joined us. She had already heard that I was on foot, and wasn't too surprised to see my dilapidated state. Just like Bill she was friendly and warm, and I felt like I was the luckiest person alive to end up in this place. Before I said good night, I asked Bill if there was any chance he could drive me back to the spot he picked me up at the next morning? I needed to continue my walk from there. He would have to take my $17, however. 'Of course, anytime after 7am. But I will not take your money', he added with a smile. I conceded, and told him again how grateful I was for his generosity. We said good night, and I went to my room.

It was as charming, comfortable and spick and span as the rest of the place. I couldn't believe that I had paid only $45 for the night in this gem of a motel. Remember the *Canton Inn*? Same price. I couldn't wait to soak in a hot bath, and it was time to take off my shoes. Gulp... My socks were stuck to the bandaids that had peeled off my heels and toes. It made for a bit of extra fun as I tried not to tear the thin skin that had filled with clear liquid in several places. 'No wonder this hurt so much', I thought. 'There are bubbles of water pressing against my shoes.' My toes were the worst. The left little one had a bag of water hanging from it, and the skin had literally peeled off the one next to it. I don't know why I didn't take any pictures - I guess it wasn't a very inspiring visual. After removing all the band aids and checking both feet, I knew the blisters had gotten worse in basically every spot. I tried not to think about having to squeeze my feet back into my shoes again the next morning, and I hoped a long bath and a good night's rest would do some healing... Soon after I was in the bath tub, trying to let my worries float away. This loving and comfortable environment would add to my recovery, I was sure. I just needed to relax and let it in.

The sheets were so soft I felt like a newborn tucking myself in. It's a good analogy, really: I felt vulnerable and clumsy, had never experienced anything like this before, was far away from everything I knew, and two people who could have been my parents had taken me in and indeed treated me like one of their own.

I might have said it out loud, or I may have spoken my words of gratitude in the stillness of my mind, but I thanked Life for the shelter and warmth it had provided me with that night.

There was only one thing out of order in the idyll of the Shawnee Motel, and that was the TV: it turned itself off several times and only came back on by itself after about 10 minutes. No remote control and no unplugging could influence this strange rhythm, and it had me wonder what could possibly cause it, as I drifted off. But then I was already in Civil War territory...

The next morning I woke, realizing I had been out like a rock the whole night. I had gotten just enough sleep to feel rested, and I had to leave early. The 8 miles I had rode in Bill's pick up the prior evening still had to be walked, and by the end of the day I needed to have done 34 miles to reach my motel in Breezewood, PA. Four more than the day prior, which had left me completely spent. 'Don't think about it', I told myself. 'One step at a time.'

I took a good look at my feet. I don't know what I had hoped for, but my blisters - though I'm sure some healing had taken place - looked just as bad as when I had gone to bed. I didn't know if to drain the ones filled with water or not. I could see the liquid was starting to turn a light yellow color, and I didn't want my skin to get inflamed on top of everything. I opened one of them. It hurt more than before, so I left it at that. The mere thought of wrapping them in a bunch of insufficient band aids again and putting on my shoes made my stomach turn. But there was no way around that until I passed a pharmacy that had higher quality band aids, which wouldn't happen until I reached Bedford, PA - 17 miles away. 'I can do it', I reassured myself. 'It's almost day 20, and once I'll cross that threshold I won't stop for anything. Come on. Here we go.'

Day 19 - planned destination: Breezewood, PA

It was about 8:15am when Bill greeted me in the office with his always friendly smile, ready to give me a ride. Thelma came to say goodbye, and I let her know that I would be passing through Schellsburg again in about two and a half hours, which was going to be the perfect time to take a break. I would see her then. She agreed, and Bill and I headed out.

After a quick stop at the town store to stock up on energy bars, bananas and Gatorade, Bill steered the pick up West on the 30 for about fifteen minutes, until we reached the spot where we had met the prior evening. He did a U-turn and stopped the car. 'The beautiful views over the next miles should help with your walk', he said. It was indeed beautiful around here as the drive had shown. And, considering the throbbing pain I already felt in my feet, I could use all the moral support I could get. 'I'll see you sometime before noon. Thank you so much for now', I told Bill. 'No problem at all', he responded. 'Are you sure you have everything you need?' I nodded gratefully. 'Okay', he said. 'I'll see you in a bit then.'

I grabbed my things, stepped out of the car and watched Bill drive off. I *did* have everything I needed as far as water, Gatorade and food was concerned, but I nonetheless felt unprepared for this day. I had pushed my body to its limits several days in a row now, and it was getting harder and harder to demand these extreme efforts from it. Dealing with the pain of the blisters added a whole other layer of challenge and, on top of that, the thought of having

166

just travelled back several miles the way I came gnawed at me. It was depressing to the mind.

My starting point was at almost 3,000 feet, and so I walked downhill for quite a while (this summit was also the highest point I came through on my journey):

The view was peaceful and serene on my way downhill:

I walked past a Bison farm - a rare sight, at least for me:

Coming into Schellsburg I took some more pictures (some sights were historic, some just caught my eye):

I was satisfied with my pace when I reached the *Shawnee Motel* and checked the time: just under two and half hours for 8 miles. Around 3.3mph, maybe even faster. 'If I can keep it up and not take more than two hours worth of breaks along the way', I thought to myself, 'I should be able to reach Breezewood not too long after sunset.'

I found Bill and Thelma outside the motel. They said I was welcome to use my room if I needed to rest (though it was already after check out time). I thanked them for the offer, but I didn't want to get too comfortable. I had to keep my mind and body set on work mode. So I asked for some ice instead, and sat down on a bench outside the motel. I put up my legs, and had some macaroni salad for lunch (not the best choice of food).

As I wrapped up and shouldered my backpack I saw Bill signaling to me, pointing to the sky in Western direction: thick storm clouds were drawing in from there. 'Great', I thought. 'Just what I need today.' Bill offered to give me a ride for another few miles, at least to where I'd be safe from the rain. But I gratefully declined. I told him and Thelma I couldn't express in words how much they had helped me, and that hopefully I would be able to come through Schellsburg again soon. Then I set out, waving to them.

I hadn't gotten far when I felt the first raindrops and no sooner had I slipped inside the poncho than it started pouring down. I tried my best to keep my feet from getting wet. The rain only lasted for about 20 minutes, and soon I was walking in bright sunshine again. I wasn't sure which was better - this was quickly turning into one of the hottest days of the whole journey so far...

I'm probably repeating myself, but I was suffering continuously that day. It was a step after step negotiation to keep going.

After 17 miles I finally came across Bedford, where a magical and precious store called CVS would be waiting for me with high quality band aids. I. Could. Not. Wait. There was a tiny problem, though: Bedford is not directly on the way. Or it is, technically, but the 30 crosses above the town and you need to get off the highway to get downtown, which would have added another mile to my already long, long day: no f***ing way. I was so spent and so frustrated and so absolutely unwilling to take even one more step than absolutely necessary, that I decided to not take the exit. But I still needed to get to the CVS that was hidden away somewhere down there, in this elusive town of Bedford, PA. So I kept walking on the 30, looking for a short cut. But the highway only kept rising higher above the town, and soon I realized that I had two choices left: walk back to the exit I hadn't taken before, which: no f***- (you know where I'm getting at) or climb over the railing and slide down a really steep 70-foot embankment that ended right by a river. Looking at that embankment worried me. I wasn't fifteen anymore, and I was in bad shape. My knees and ankles were weak and stiff, and - even more importantly in this instance - my wrists were still shot from the scooter. I still wasn't able to put any weight on them, beyond an absolute minimum. And now I was going to slide down this hill on my hands and butt, risking to injure who knows what next? 'God, get me down there safely with nothing worse than dirty shorts', I thought, before I sat down in the sand and let my weight carry me downhill. Trees and bushes helped with the task as I grasped onto anything that slowed me down enough to stay in control. For a blink of an eye the possibility of hidden thorns tearing open my skin terrified me, but then I had already reached the bottom, safe and in one piece. Phew. I wiped the dirt off my clothes. The river had a narrow concrete crossing here, and there was a park on the other side. Once there, it would be less than half a mile to the CVS, according to Google maps.

I passed a family - a father with his two sons - who were out here fishing, and said *hello*. They greeted me back, but looked confused at this guy stepping out of the thicket, which led nowhere but straight up to the highway...

Downtown Bedford had some pretty architecture. I considered taking pictures, but then I couldn't make myself do anything more than walk to the CVS and sit down somewhere to get lunch. The heat was brutal now, and the final never-ending 0.3 miles struck again... The last few hundred feet I walked through a meadow, hoping for the slightest relief the softer ground might provide for me. I almost ended up hurting my ankle when my foot suddenly disappeared in a hole in the grass, but I was lucky. And then the automated sliding doors of the Bedford CVS finally opened in front of me: what a glorious feeling!

172

About fifteen minutes later I sat down outside the adjacent Burger King, with a lunch meal, stocked up on Gatorade, some ice to cool my legs, and enough proper band aids to last for a while. I took off my shoes to give my feet some fresh air while eating. They were dirty and sticky - just like the rest of me. I couldn't help but feel embarrassed at the looks of people coming in and out of the restaurant. An older couple asked where I was going, and if I needed a ride. I told them Breezewood was my destination, but unfortunately I couldn't accept their offer. I had to walk the distance, that was the whole point. The man looked in that direction, and then back at me with concern. 'You know that's 18 miles from here, right?' I told him I knew, and that I wish it wasn't that far, but that I should be able to get there by latest 9 or 10pm. The couple wished me good luck, and left. 'God, what am I doing?' I thought to myself once more. 'This is nuts.'

I received Wi-Fi from the Burger King and decided to do a quick livestream on my Facebook page. I hadn't done an update for a day, because where I had come through there was simply no network connection. Getting instant support from about two dozen people, who were following my journey, was wonderful. Everyone was so encouraging. I lamented about the ordeal of the last couple of days, and that the best way to describe the pain in my feet was that they felt like I had razorblades in my socks, mixed with glowing coals. When I watch that video clip now, I'm surprised at how relaxed and at ease I look. Because I know inside I felt nothing but fatigue and dread at the time.

After I said goodbye to my loyal Facebook companions I went about replacing the band aids, which was time consuming and fickle. And when I was finally done, I felt little difference putting my shoes back on: it still hurt way too much. I told myself that at least the blisters would heal better now as I grabbed my backpack and got to my feet, ready (or not) to tackle the second half of the day.

Not an hour later I was lying on my back in the grass beside the highway, with nothing left in my body... I had been walking down the slowly declining 30, noticing more and more the intense heat burning down on my back. It suddenly felt unbearable! I had willed the sun to disappear behind some clouds (which miraculously worked for a few minutes), and then my strength left me, just like that. I had stumbled on for a few hundred feet more, before stripping off the backpack and letting myself drop onto the ground. Now I was on my back, breathing hard, completely exhausted. 'I have no time for this', I remember thinking. 'I'm already pushing it with the mileage. Ten minutes, then I have to continue.' But it didn't feel like that would be enough. I drank and ate something, and then lay back down again, trying to calm my mind. 'Don't panic', I told myself. 'Check in with your body. Breathe.' I took a few slow and very conscious breaths, giving my system a chance to reboot, and then hopefully recover.

Whenever I feel the need to heal in some way, I become very still in mind and body. It's almost like pressing a pause button and then staying in that space. I focus and sort of wander through the body, like I'm scanning it with a warm light, breathing deeply and slowly. It palpably raises the vibration in my body, and reduces stress and discomfort. Really, it's a very focused meditation. And it certainly helped me through this physical low.

As I sat back up, willing myself to continue on, a car pulled up on the shoulder not far ahead. A young guy got out, walked over and asked if I needed a ride, or some water or something. I was very moved by this gesture. It doesn't happen a lot that someone just stops on the highway and offers to give a stranger a ride - that much I had learned by now. I said that I really appreciated it, but that I had to keep walking. I asked his name. It was Andrew, if I remember correctly. We shook hands, then he got back in his car and his girlfriend waved out the window as they drove off. For all I know this compassionate encounter did as much to revive me as my meditation.

It was after 6pm when I came through at town called Everett,

PA. I stocked up on water and Gatorade at a gas station. I remember thinking how merciless the heat was for this time of day and, sure enough, when I walked through downtown Everett a sign outside a shop showed 90 degrees in the shade. 'Jesus', I thought. 'No wonder I almost collapsed before. It was likely over 110 in the sun back there...' I decided then and there that I would get a hat and sunglasses at the next possible location. It was clearly way over due at this point.

Everett also had the only Bernie yard sign I saw on my walk (not surprising, since most people had given up hope that Bernie could still be the nominee at this point):

The day started to cool down now, and I still had the hardest part ahead of me: breaking the 30 mile threshold and making it through the 4 to follow. Apparently, that wasn't enough of a challenge, however: overall, the landscape had been getting more and more volatile with changing elevation, and the last stretch of this day was a steep uphill...

I was about a mile and a half out now. I had put on my headlamp a few minutes earlier, and this time it wasn't just to warn drivers of my position - I couldn't see a thing without it. It was near pitch black walking up this mountain, and - other than my GPS - I had no way to tell how far I was from my destination. Occasionally a car or a truck passed me, but their beams lit up the surroundings for mere moments, and then it was back to darkness. I might as well have been a hundred miles from the next town.

When I finally saw lights ahead on the top of this climb, I was incredibly relieved. It felt like reaching a proper mountain pass. Breezewood's stores and gas stations became visible in the distance and my motel was now in relatively close reach, when I noticed a laundromat on the left side of the road. Its door was wide open, and it looked like a kind of self-service place that was open 24/7. I knew I had to do my laundry soon - if not that day then certainly the day after - and this seemed like a perfect opportunity. But more than clean clothes I needed to rest... I silently debated with myself. The motel was another 0.3 miles down the road, and I considered going there first and then coming back. But that would add 0.6 miles to an already very long day. On the other hand, staying here at the laundromat until my clothes were washed and dried would take me at least 45 minutes, if I cut the cycles short. I couldn't bear the thought of delaying my arrival at the motel by almost an hour. It would be nearly 11pm before I could ice my legs and rest.

I actually started walking for the motel, then turned back after a few steps, then turned around again - I was so torn. Eventually I decided to stay, and get it done as quickly as I could. I changed in the bathroom there and threw my laundry in the washer. Then I sat down on a bench, and put up my legs. I was completely exhausted. Sitting there alone in this laundromat that seemed to have no supervision or staff, dressed in nothing but sweatpants and a windbreaker, with the hard florescent light and the monotonous sounds of the washing machine, I felt like in some parallel world. It was a strange experience.

Fifty minutes later and with clean clothes in tow, I tackled the last 0.3 miles. As always, they were a pure joyride... Not.

The relief at reaching the *Wiltshire Motel* was great, even compared to most other days. With the added detour through Bedford I probably had done over 35 miles. Then there was the heat. It had been a tough day, and I knew I deserved every minute of rest I could get.

Once in my room I was shocked at how skinny I had gotten. Hot water was filling the bathtub as I got undressed and I suddenly stopped, startled, looking at myself in the mirror. My face was gaunt, and I could make out bones on my back that I had not seen since I was a little kid. 'The constant up and down is really making my body burn through its reserves', I realized. The weight loss had definitely accelerated over the past days. Even on the scooter, when I was in a higher pulse range, I had not shed pounds like this.

I didn't have a scale then, and the first time I got to weigh myself was back in Los Angeles ten days later. I was still 15 pounds below my normal weight at that point, even though I had stopped walking for over a week. So that night I must have easily been 20 pounds under, somewhere around 145 lbs, probably less.

After my nightly bath, I watched a little TV and found some comfort and motivation in the many encouraging comments and posts people left me on Facebook. And then there were some that worried me: people living in Pennsylvania told me that the temperatures would only go up in the coming days. I had another 34 miles ahead of me the following day. Any thought about besting that in the condition I was in, was discouraging and pointless. 'Just go to sleep', I told myself. 'Tomorrow is a new day.' And so I crawled underneath the sheets (always my favorite part of the day) and closed my eyes, surrendering to the hope that everything would work out somehow.

Day 20 - planned destination: St. Thomas, PA

When I woke up I could already feel it: it was going to be a hot, hot day. But something else made me forget about the heat almost instantly, and that was the fact that - to my complete and utter delight - my blisters weren't hurting as much as the days prior, when I slipped into my shoes. I estimated the pain was about 30% less, which meant that I was healing, and it would only get better from here on. Yipeee! I felt like a kid in a candy store.

I made my way to the first gas station to stock up on liquids and food, and then headed straight for a souvenir store where I got myself a camouflage-themed Pittsburgh Steelers sun hat, and a pair of sunglasses. It cost me over $50, which hurt, but there was no way I was going to make it through this day without protection from the sun. And, good Lord, was it already burning down at 9am...

The hat and shades worked wonders. I can't stress enough the relief they gave me. I know this seems obvious to most people, I just never wear hats or shades in my personal life, and so this was kind of a novelty for me.

Of all the parts of Pennsylvania I travelled through, this day's stretch was the most hilly: it was a never-ending up and down from start to finish, and even with my new protection I was still desperately trying to stay out of the sun. The good thing about being in wild and hilly country was that there where almost always trees on both sides, and a lot of the time they were high enough to create some shade on either the left or right shoulder.

And so I walked along, uphill or downhill, frequently crossing the road, seeking shade like a vampire-wanderer... I remember the short relief I felt every time I was in between an incline and decline. Uphill tested my stamina, and I could hardly drink fast enough to keep up with sweating, but as soon as the incline was behind me I had to deal with the stress walking downhill put on my joints. The phrase 'what goes up, must come down' became very apparent to me in those days.

As I mentioned, I never stopped drinking and I went through my half gallon of water and two bottles of Gatorade in no time. Which soon turned out to be a problem. There was nothing around here - no stores or gas stations where I could stock up on supplies - not until I would reach the city of McConnellsburg, 19 miles into my day. So when I saw a young Amish woman and an older lady work outside a property somewhere in the middle of nowhere, I didn't hesitate for long before I removed my hat and shades and approached them: 'I'm sorry to disturb you, M'am. Is there any way I could fill up my hydration pack? I'm low on water, and I can't see any stores or gas stations on my path anytime soon.' The lady - Pat was her name - waved me over. She told me that there was indeed nothing around here, and it was a good idea of me to ask. 'I'll get you some bottled water', she said. 'It's better than from the tap.' She soon came back with the water and made sure that I filled the hydration pack up all the way. I told her I was very appreciative of her help, and that I would like to at least pay her for the water. It wasn't hard to see that she wasn't swimming in money. I handed her four singles, but she refused. I said it would make me feel better, and she smiled and said: 'Okay, I'll take one dollar, but that's it.' So I handed her a single dollar and thanked her for her generosity. Before I left she warned me not to walk into the night: 'There are bears in this area.' I promised to be careful, and set out.

Several hours later I was excited to finally reach McConnellsberg:

It had been a long way downhill into this valley. My knees and
ankles were killing me, and lunch at 19 miles into the day was
really pushing it. I was hungrier than ever, and needed something
real to eat. I don't know why I was craving pizza, but that's what I
decided on, and so I stopped at a pizzeria halfway through town.

Would you like to you know how nice it was to sit in an air conditioned space, eating fresh cheese pizza and slurping an ice cold Arnold Palmer, after walking 19 miles up and down the hills of Pennsylvania, in 93 degrees in the shade? I'll tell you: very nice. Very, very, very nice. The only problem was, I had about 30 minutes before I had to step outside again and keep doing the same for another 15 miles. 'Don't think about that right now', a voice inside my head whispered and brought me back into the moment. 'Hm, this pizza is delicious.'

After my lunch break I discovered something that would make me choose Italy's most famous food export every time I had the opportunity in the days following: pizza is nothing short of miraculous superfood! Heading out of town I soon faced another steep incline - no surprise there. But this one was on the steeper and longer end of the spectrum, even for Pennsylvania. *9% incline for the next 3 1/2 miles* a road sign told me. That sounded and looked like a lot, and I was worried. I didn't know how I would deal with such a challenge, rested or not. Well, here's how I dealt with it: I walked it like a young mountain goat! I couldn't believe how my body suddenly functioned almost by itself. It felt like I was being pulled on a string, like I had shifted into my 9%-uphill-gear and I had to do nothing but watch. It was an incredible feeling. As I marched uphill with a pace so steady and strong that it would have put a San Francisco street car to shame, I realized that this resulted from several things: the pizza gave me momentary strength, no doubt. But I had also trained my body in walking uphill over the last days, and the 20 pounds I had lost made a huge difference, as well.

Then came the turning point:

Now it was 3 1/2 miles *down* the other side, and that was tough. All the other joints aside, there was a lot of pressure resting on my toes. The nasty sting I had felt before in the ball of my large left toe returned, and I had no idea what to do about it. So I settled on hoping it wouldn't get worse.

Heading downhill here also had its upsides, however (I really needed a wide-angle camera to capture the visual, but I hope you can see it anyway):

I call this *American Jungle*. That's what kept coming into my head, anyway. I wasn't surprised that Pat had told me earlier bears lived in the area. Of course they did. Every animal typical for this climate would live here. It was pure wilderness as far as the eye could see, with the one little concrete road curving through it. I was reminded of the wildness of nature and its uncompromising laws. If someone were to get lost in these mountains, stuck with a broken leg and no phone signal or battery, they would very likely die. It might sound banal and maybe that's not a revelation to anyone, but as I was walking through these parts I was reminded very vividly of how humans are (physically) pretty small beings, who are incredibly reliant on their intellect and modern technology, and we've forgotten much about our animal nature and our connection to our original mother, our planet. American Jungle... It's a good movie title, if nothing else.

Later that day - it was close to sunset - I made an encouraging observation as I looked out over the flat land ahead: I had put the mountains behind me! Ahh, it was a sweet, sweet feeling to walk on a level road again. And, as the knowledge of having put a difficult chapter on this journey behind me sunk in, I allowed myself a bold and encouraging thought, and shared it with my Facebook followers:

For the first time I dare to believe I'm gonna make it.

And - even if there was no certainty, of course - believing I could was a glorious feeling. Additionally, my feet (my blisters, at least) were barely hurting at this point, which was the best thing I could even think of, and to put icing on the cake, I saw more fireflies that night. And this time in even greater numbers than back in Kalida, OH... Thousands lit up all across a huge meadow to the left of the road, and I was once again standing and watching in awe. The view silenced my mind, and made me appreciate life for the gift it is. If only these little bugs were bright enough to capture in a photograph (I really tried), but this will have to remain an image in my memory alone.

So yeah, things were pretty good all around at that moment, and I thought to myself that I might be reaching the light at the end of this tunnel. But things rarely stay the same for long, right? Change is the only constant, we all know that to be true. And so my inspired walk came to a sudden halt when I arrived at the

184

address Google maps had provided me with for the *Travel Inn Motel,* and there was nothing around me. Some sort of farm back there in the dark, yes, but no motel. No residences, either. Nothing. I checked once more to see if this really was the right address, and it was. I anxiously scanned the surroundings, a familiar feeling of panic growing in my chest. This area was as rural as it got, and this was the end of my day. I had walked 34 miles, and was now dead tired and alone in the dark. I had nowhere to go if this motel didn't exist...

Fear grips you with remarkable power sometimes. I simply couldn't think of a harmless explanation to this. I couldn't imagine that maybe the address was wrong after all, and the *Travel Inn Motel* was a little further up the road. All I knew in this moment was that Google maps showed me I had arrived, and in fact I hadn't. I couldn't think beyond what my eyes saw. And that was dark, merciless night in every direction. My heart pumped adrenalin and other fear-triggered hormones through my body, and I knew I had to keep my head straight. 'Keep walking', I told myself. And I did, suddenly much faster than before. Then I saw a house on the right side of the road. There was a light on and, coming closer, I made out two people sitting on the porch. 'Excuse me', I immediately blurted out in my best I-know-I'm-a-complete-stranger-walking-out-of-the-dark-late-at-night-but-I-swear-I'm-harmless voice. 'My GPS tells me that the *Travel Inn Motel* is back there, but there's nothing. Would you know-' I didn't get to finish my question. 'The *Travel Inn* is less than half a mile up the road on the right, just keep going', the man interrupted me. 'Oh, okay', I sighed in relief. 'Thank you so much! I was getting a little worried there for a second.' I laughed like a big dork and waved, quickly moving on. And indeed, after about 0.4 miles the motel materialized out of the dark, like some good wizard had decided to save me from night and cold with his magic spell. The little things (though, I guess survival isn't that little) can be truly wonderful.

I was in good spirits that night. It had been one of the best days so far on this journey, following some very tough days. Feeling physically strong coming out of McConnellsburg had given me confidence, and I had enough energy to do a livestream on Facebook to share the experiences of my day. The encouraging feedback I once again received from the people who followed my walk only confirmed my feeling from earlier: I was going to make it, and things would surely be much easier from here on out...

Day 21 - planned destination: Gettysburg, PA

I set out on July 20th, having decided to take a minor detour that day: my next stop would be Gettysburg. It added a mile or two to my overall journey, but this walk was in support of Bernie Sanders, after all, who had quoted Abraham Lincoln many times in his speeches. With my blisters being on the mend I also felt more confident about my physical state, and who knew when I would be getting the next chance to see this historic city? It seemed like the right thing to do.

I remember two things about walking that day: one, it was really hot, and two, I listened to music for the first and only time. My good friend Eva back in Austria had posted a song on my Facebook wall, a cover version of Simon & Garfunkel's 'The Sound of Silence' by the band Disturbed, to show support for my journey. And I loved it so much, I couldn't stop listening to it. Though it was usually one of the first things people asked me about whenever I told anyone of my walk, I had never considered listening to music or audiobooks or anything of that sort. It was clear to me from the very beginning that I wanted to have an undisturbed (pun not intended) experience of whatever would happen during it. Music, especially vocal music with lyrics, is a strong emotional stimuli, and it would have created another experience in my psyche on top of the one I was out there having already, and diminish its power. But for this one day I allowed myself to fully indulge. You should listen to the song if you can: it starts out quietly, like a whisper, and masterfully builds to an intense and gripping crescendo. I loved the singer's voice, it really pulled me into whatever story he was telling. And - you probably guessed it - I cried. Like I said, music does things to you, and soon grand fantasies sprung from the depth of my imagination, dramatically underscored by the song:

I reached Philadelphia, where the roads were lined with people. They all recognized me, and cheered me on as I limped the last mile. I could see John-Michael, who grinned happily as he filmed my arrival - ever the filmmaker. His partner Becca came running, hugging me enthusiastically, while trying not to stop my walk. 'You made it!' she shouted. I was so grateful to see my friends, but managed only to cringe as I tried to smile back, knowing I still had to finish the last stretch. And then, as I looked up, I saw with surprise that Bernie Sanders himself was waiting farther ahead. He had learned about my walk and wanted to personally thank me. 'This is the most honorable moment of my life', I knew.

Tears ran into my eyes as I finally stepped before this great man, barely able to stand from the pain in my legs and feet. He grabbed me by the shoulders, and looked me up and down like a proud father. Then he firmly shook my hand, moved that someone had gone to such lengths to prove that true integrity and standing up for what's right, whatever the cost - the core values of his life - were not just a myth anymore.

Later I walked next to Senator Sanders during the march, and at the end he called me up to the podium with him to speak about my journey, thanking me again for my sacrifice. Thousands applauded and cheered. It was like electricity in the air - everyone knew we were here to witness an incredible moment in time. And in the days following, tens of thousands of protesters took a stand in the streets of Philadelphia, ready to fight for democracy and justice, and - seeing the powerful unity of the people - the Democratic party was left with no other choice but to elect Bernie Sanders as the Democratic nominee. He went on to become the 45th President of the United States, which triggered a profound shift in America and the rest of the world, ringing in a new era of healing and peace, as humans rediscovered their

188

compassion, and the deep interconnectedness of all life. We had turned the ship around - what a glorious time to be alive!

Alright, back to reality (sad emoji here).

I'm embarrassed to share this fantasy, but it's connected to something I mentioned earlier: I needed to believe somewhere deep down that what I did was meaningful, and day dreams like these - however ridiculous and ego-inflated - helped me push through excruciating and seemingly hopeless moments. Many of them. Sometimes it really is necessary to dream without boundaries...

At just about that time another potential challenge announced itself: my right Achilles tendon started to hurt. This was a new one for me. Just like the shin splints and the stress fracture before, I had never injured my achilles or done anything to cause it to hurt. I was worried. This tendon is such a large and essential part of the foot and the process of walking, that I wasn't sure how to deal with it. I certainly couldn't afford it to get worse. I had an average of 32 miles to walk every day to make it to Philly in time. I didn't want to risk an injury, so I fell into a slight limp, taking weight off my right leg, which momentarily helped. Naturally, I now had more weight on my left foot, and soon the ball of my large toe made itself known with a loud and clear *f*** you!*

After my frustration about its rebellion subsided, I turned to a tactic I had been using on and off for a while now, which was talking to it. Literally. Similarly to the healing meditation I described earlier, I tried to connect in a very direct sense with whatever part of my feet or legs were hurting - only while walking, instead of lying down. I focused on where the stinging pain was coming from, and said the following (or a variation thereof): 'I know this is hard. We're going through something very difficult, and you're doing an incredible job. Thank you for being such a trooper. You have every right to hurt. It's okay. It's gonna be over soon, I promise...' It might sound funny, but I'll be damned if it didn't help. Pain is the body's way of telling you that something isn't the way it's supposed to be. Of course, that can range from barely noticeable low level warning signs, such as minor muscle tension, to bright red blinking life-or-death alert when, for example, your arm is ripped off, or something extreme like that. Sometimes pain is telling you, that if you don't stop doing what you're doing, there will be consequences and a lot more pain, like in the case of my stress fracture, which clearly communicated to me that a real fracture would be next if I didn't listen. Other pain is less urgent, I found, and all it needs is to be acknowledged and then it will let you be for a while. And so it was with the ball of my large left toe.

My achilles, it seemed, wasn't getting worse, but the dull pain and weakness persisted. I remembered that Michael Gibino had been struggling with a bad achilles a few days prior, and I reached out to him for any advice he might have. He told me to use KT tape, and gave me detailed instructions on how to apply it. I still had one strip of tape left from treating my shin splints earlier in my journey, and so I took a quick break and did just as Michael told me: I attached the tape to the sole of my foot on the inside of my heel, and then pulled it up alongside the achilles, giving it a good stretch before attaching it to my calf muscle. And it worked like a charm. My right achilles never gave me trouble again. My left one was a different story, but I didn't know that at this point...

It was late in the afternoon when I was nearing Gettysburg, and it was hard to imagine that I could be more exhausted than I was. The heat had really punished me that day, and yet the little boy in me, who had always been hanging on his grandfather's lips when he was telling stories from World War II, was fascinated as I passed remnants and memorials from the Civil War:

190

A defining chapter in the history of the United States had taken place in and around this city. The energy of it still lingered. Maybe because it is kept alive by us through stories, art, reenactments, etc., but it was almost palpable.

I pushed myself forward, knowing I would take a dinner break soon, and that on that night I would be given a special treat (a first and only on my journey): earlier, I had reached out to Bernie supporters, inquiring if anyone in the Gettysburg area would be able to give me a ride into town that night. I needed to walk a few miles past Gettysburg to make my average, but the challenging motel situation required that I would have to come back into the city. A man named Bruce had responded and said he'd love to help out. He had even extended an invitation to stay at his house instead of a motel. He had told me his wife Jeanne and he would love to put me up to show their support. I had gladly accepted the generous offer and said I'd let him know later how far I would make it, so that we could agree on a meeting point. Again, I was moved by how Bernie supporters took care of each other.

I finally reached the city center. Gettysburg is beautiful. The history, the architecture, the statues. It reminded me of Europe. Growing up, I was used to city walls and other structures that dated back to the 13th century or more. Few places in the US, especially on the West Coast, have history comparable to that. And history is what gives a city its character. I felt a familiarity here. It gave me strength, somehow. I sought out the Wills house where the original statues of Abraham Lincoln and the civilian - the ones I had seen earlier in Warsaw, IN - are placed. President Lincoln had slept in the Wills house the night before his immortal address:

I then sat down on a bench in the shade, letting Abraham Lincoln's famous words *Of the people, by the people, for the people* sink in. It wasn't an accident that Bernie Sanders quoted them in his speeches: they were the golden rule of Democratic government.

I felt inspired to share some thoughts about this on my page, and recorded a video. I felt more strongly than ever that Lincoln's words were not applied anymore in US politics - not by a long stretch. The government wasn't of, by, and for the people: the government was of, by and for big corporations, banks, special interests and billionaires. President Obama had said recently that people shouldn't believe that the system was rigged, it would only make them bitter. According to him, the system wasn't rigged. It was all just a big conspiracy. That's a laughable statement if you look at the current situation in the US government: we know congress passes federal laws, and federal laws impact every person living in the country. Thus, Congress' highest priority should be to make sure that laws are written and passed according to the will of the majority of the more than 300 million people living in the US (the people who elected them into office to begin with to represent their interests), right? But that's not the case.

What's happening instead is that Congress members' votes are literally bought by the financial elite via the travesty and insanity of the lobbying system. Which means there is no democracy. The people's interests are not represented. And instead only the interests of corporations, banks, special interests and billionaires, who - more often than not - have a hand in writing bills. And that's not a rigged system? That is the *definition* of a rigged system, if you ask me. And, in my opinion, it is this circumstance that is the cancer at the core of almost all the big issues this country is facing, be it wars, student debt, military spending, health care, education, drug prices, the environment, prisons for profit - you name it. All of these big money industries are lobbying the government. Which means they literally pay the people, who decide which laws will pass or not, to vote in *their* favor and not in favor of the public - namely the people. (remember the first three words in the constitution: *WE THE PEOPLE...*) This leads to laws, which ensure these companies' profits are prioritized, and the interests of the people - who should be represented by their *representatives* - fall by the wayside.

And who was the one candidate in this presidential race who not only understood this problem fully and completely, but also was willing and ready to fight this rigged system, and get big money out of politics? Bernie Sanders, of course. And how committed to this was he? So committed that he ran his entire campaign from the ground up only on donations from average people like you and me. Because he understood that if you take money from big corporations, banks, special interests and billionaires, you are beholden to them. No one hands out millions of dollars to a presidential candidate without the mutual understanding that once that candidate is in office, they will return the favor. *No one.* And who was the candidate who not only took any big money you can think of in support of her campaign, but also has deep ties to virtually every one of the industries that lobby Congress day in, day out? Hillary Clinton. And that, in my opinion, was the crux of it all: Bernie Sanders understood that without stopping big money from influencing the government, *nothing would ever really change*. Nothing essential and nothing meaningful. Only superficialities would be fixed here and there, to put people's minds at ease and give them the illusion that there's progress. Hillary Clinton, on the other hand, was so deeply embedded in this pay for play system, that even if she had suddenly come to and acknowledged this crucial issue, she would probably not have been able to do anything about it. It's pretty obvious she and her husband have been building these relationships for decades, and it doesn't take a lot of imagination to understand that there must be a lot of debt and owed favors going both ways.

I shared my video, and went to have dinner at a hot dog place around the corner. I got some enthusiastic support regarding my cause from the young guys working at the hot dog place, and I set out well-fed and ready to take on a few more miles.

It was already getting dark when I left the city behind. It had been more than 29 miles so far from the *Travel Inn Motel*, and I could feel that 34 or 35 wasn't in the running tonight. I was just too tired. I looked up Google maps and chose a spot that would end my day on a little more than 32 miles. I texted Bruce the coordinates, and he agreed to pick me up at around 9:30pm.

I was utterly spent when I finally recognized the street I had chosen as my end point for the day. Just in time Bruce's car pulled up, and I was surprised to see he hadn't come alone: his wife Jeanne was with him. While this was certainly an unusual kind of meeting - I could tell that both Bruce and Jeanne (who had slipped on one of her Bernie shirts before getting in the car) naturally felt a bit awkward picking up a perfect stranger on the side of the highway at night - I couldn't have been happier. I don't know how many times I expressed my thanks. These people were already heroes to me. I told them just a little about my day, and in turn they entrusted me with how their grown daughters had advised them against picking up some stranger, who might murder them in their sleep. We laughed about it, and after about 15 minutes we pulled into their garage.

196

Their home was beautiful. Warm and cozy, with pictures of their children and grandchildren hanging on the walls. A real family place. And I was treated like family, too. I quickly shed my embarrassment over how dirty I was, and after a bath, Jeanne, Bruce and I sat down together in their living room - all the while icing my legs - and had what I can only describe as a wonderful time. The conversations about Bernie Sanders and how much we needed him in this country were inspiring and encouraging. These people got it. And so did many others out there. I remembered I wasn't alone. But there was more. Jeanne and Bruce listened with an open heart. We laughed together and bonded. I felt that, despite being a stranger, they sincerely cared about my wellbeing, my health and safety, and I knew I could have asked for nearly anything, and they would have done their best to provide it. I think deep down they understood that what I did came from a place of caring, as well. They felt that it had value. And they wanted to support it as much as they could.

I enjoyed myself so much, and felt so comfortable in their company, that I overlooked the time and ended up getting less sleep than I usually did. I didn't think this would be an issue at the time, but my body would soon let me know the price for my carelessness...

When I got out of bed the next morning delicious coffee and breakfast was waiting for me. Bruce and Jeanne had gotten up early to make sure I had everything I needed before setting out:

Jeanne handed me a brand-new blue Bernie T-shirt as a goodbye gift, and she let me know that I was always welcome in their home, should I come through Gettysburg again. And I knew she meant it.

I don't remember the context of the conversation Bruce and I had during the fifteen minutes together in the car, but he said something profound regarding human nature, and it stuck with me: 'Everyone believes they're doing the right thing. *Everyone*.' I remember thinking that this was something many people in the world have not come to understand, and I was grateful for his insight. It reminded me that - at the end of the day - humanity is in this together. Even if we disagree with people, and even if we know for sure they are wrong - we're all just trying our best, according to where we are at on our own path...

Bruce stopped the car. We were back at the spot he and Jeanne had picked me up the night before, and where I would continue my walk today. Once again it was time to say goodbye, and just like before with Crimson, Tawnie and Blaire, Erin and CeyShon, and Jessica, Cadence and Preston, it was hard. Bruce and Jeanne had taken care of me and - connected through the deep values Bernie Sanders embodied and brought out in us all - even a short time together left an impact and was meaningful. These people were my friends now. What we all went through together on a larger level throughout this election, and the way they had taken part in a special moment in my life, meant I would never forget them. Bruce and I hugged, and I promised I would keep him posted about my progress. We shared a smile, then I set out.

Day 22 - planned destination: York, PA

It was going to be another hot day, that much was clear: it wasn't even 8am yet and it was already in the 80s. Still, I felt confident that this leg of my journey wouldn't be too much of a challenge. Due to the early start, there would be plenty of time for breaks, and that would allow me to take it a bit easier overall. It wouldn't take long to find out that *easy* wasn't in the cards for that day, however, and that I would need all the extra time and then some to make it through...

Currently things were going well. At least physically. After the pleasant imagery of Gettysburg and the jungle-like forests before that, the stretch I was on now was among the ugliest of my entire walk. Basically, the 30 became a narrow countryside highway. It was a lot of traffic squeezed into insufficient space, and most of what I remember is being frustrated at the deafening engine sounds, the lack of trees lining the road where I would usually find some shade, and the fact that the narrow shoulders on both sides fell off in a steep angle, creating the most uncomfortable walking experience possible. One of the highlights of this day was a banner I saw outside the Emmanuel United Church of Christ in Abbottstown:

That. All of that. Let those be the rules.

Another thing that helped me push forward - you could call it a little tactical trump up my sleeve - was that I knew I was about to break a crucial threshold: today I would be in the double digits for the first time, as far as remaining miles were concerned. I was excited like a kid and kept checking Google maps to see when the remaining distance would drop below 100 miles, and then it did:

I proudly shared the news on my page. This meant that I had already put 634 miles behind me! Double digits seemed absolutely doable. I mean, 99 miles were a walk in the park compared to the overall 734, right? 'Bring it on, you ugly, hot, uncomfortable day', I thought confidently. 'I've got you by the ba-' And then, without warning, my left Achilles turned to stone...

I had slept too little, I already told you. And I instantly knew this was the result. I pulled up my leg in surprise and dread. I had never felt anything like it. I could hardly step on my heel. It wasn't a subtle pain like I had felt in my right achilles the day before, this was an all out you're-done-walking signal my body gave me. I prayed I hadn't injured myself. But even if I hadn't, I knew this wasn't something I would just be able to brush off. So I very, very carefully limped to the closest place that had some grass and shade - which was an eternity away, around 0.3 miles - and I somehow got there.

With extraordinary care I removed my backpack and sat down behind the fence. This was private property, but I couldn't worry about trespassing right now. I took off my shoes and just tried to relax my feet and my legs as I messaged Michael Gibino. He quickly responded and told me to massage the calf muscle, put up the leg and tape it like I had done on the other side, before continuing. 'Sorry, man. I know it sucks', he empathized. 'But there's nothing else you can do at the moment.' I thanked him and went back to taking care of myself. I laid down in the grass with my legs up, once again going through my self-healing meditation. It calmed me, and deepened my breath. All I could do now was hope that the tape would have the same effect it had had the day before.

I pulled out the new roll of tape I had gotten at a pharmacy earlier. As I unrolled it I started to wonder about the material. 'This doesn't feel like the other tape I used', I thought to myself. And when I tried to apply it and saw that this tape neither stretched nor properly stuck to my skin, I realized I had bought the wrong kind. 'Jesus Christ, what now?' I thought in despair. As much as I massaged it and talked to it, acknowledging the pain in hopes of lessening it - the tendon didn't want to release. It was hard, tight and extremely tender. And to make matters worse, I was somewhere in rural Pennsylvania, with no pharmacy that would carry KT tape anywhere close by... I decided to rest for 30 minutes in the shade, and then try to continue.

When I dragged myself back out onto the road I immediately went back to limping: nothing had changed. My foot just wouldn't do what I needed it to do. My achilles was like a stick of wood attached to my calf muscle. I couldn't put weight on it, and certainly not push off the ground with any real momentum. 'Oh my God', I thought. 'I've got another 17 miles ahead of me...' How on Earth was I going to make it like this? Even if I did the absolute minimum, I needed to walk another 14 or 15 at the very least to have anything close to a chance of making it to Philadelphia for Bernie's march on the 24th. 'I'm so screwed...'

And this is what the rest of my day looked like: I walked for about an hour at a time (at this point a distance of around 2 miles), sometimes less, and then took a break wherever I would find shade. I first massaged my calf muscle and drank as much as I could, then I put my legs up against a fence or a ledge or whatever else I could find, and tried to let it all go. The heat, the pain, the frustration, the unappealing surroundings, thoughts about what lay ahead... I focused on my breath, and felt the movement of my chest rising and falling. The air filling my lungs. After ten or fifteen minutes I continued, each time hoping for the tightness to go away. And it never did. There was, however, a sort of truce that my achilles agreed to, once it realized that I wouldn't stop walking. The terms seemed to be that things wouldn't get worse, if I kept going at snail pace for the rest of the way.

It was a rough day. There's nothing like having to literally limp along an ugly highway all day in 90+ degrees in the shade, with no shade anywhere in sight...

The sun began to set when I finally reached the city of York. The *Modernaire Motel* I had called earlier to reserve a room, was at the other end of it. Like before in Massillon, OH, people here looked tough. It was expressed in their clothes, their tattoos, the way they walked, their hardened features. Maybe it wasn't a dangerous atmosphere I felt, but certainly a rough and angry one. And poverty wherever I looked. At the same time there was history and some beautiful architecture, and this mix made York an intriguing place in my experience. It inhabited a lot of struggle, but also had a strong and vibrant pulse.

After 27 miles I finally called it quits: the constant limping had caused my left foot to tense up, and now the stinging pain inside the ball of my large toe was so strong, I sucked in air and cringed whenever it hit me, which was every couple of minutes. I stopped where I was and called an Uber.

A few minutes later my driver pulled up, and I was granted the glorious experience of sitting in a soft car seat. What a treat! After 3 miles we stopped at a CVS right across the street from my motel. I asked my driver to wait, nonetheless. I couldn't bear the thought of taking even one step more than was absolutely necessary. I stocked up on Gatorade, band aids, epsom salts and KT tape (all my hopes for the days ahead rested on it) and then the Uber delivered me at the *Modernaire Motel*.

It was a charming little place, and the owner friendly and accommodating. I took a bunch of ice with me after I paid, and went straight across the parking lot to my room. It was still somewhat light out. I hoped that the longer turnaround time, a hot bath, and lots of ice would give my achilles a chance to recover enough to continue the next day. But there was no guarantee for that: I had walked 12 miles on it, and virtually all of it on concrete, when the sensible thing to do would have been to stop.

An hour later I was watching TV, my achilles resting on a bag of ice, while munching on cheese pizza I had gotten delivered to my room. It was Heaven compared to what I gone through earlier, but I couldn't help feeling anxious. The fact aside, that the next morning I'd have to drive back the 3 miles to pick up where I had stopped - I was really close to making it now. Only 89 miles left to the Wells Fargo Center in Philly. The possibility of my achilles not getting better left me restless and worried... There was nothing I could do aside from getting a good amount of sleep, and leave the rest up to fate.

Day 23 - planned destination: Ronks, PA

In the morning I felt rested. After a hot shower and a quick styrofoam cup of coffee, I applied the KT tape along my achilles on both legs (just to be sure), and packed up my things. Then I called an Uber, and a few minutes later I was back at the street corner I had stopped walking the day before.

The first steps out of the motel earlier had given me hope: my achilles seemed to have released much of the tension over night, and now it was all about the tape doing its job and keeping it that way. Still, I was extremely careful on the first stretch. I was on high alert with every step, consciously following each movement, checking in with any part of my body that could give me trouble. After about a mile of walking like this through the streets of York, I felt fairly confident that my achilles would be fine, and so I fell into a more relaxed stride. It was such a relief. Like I said earlier, the thought of an injury stopping me this close to my destination had given me serious anxiety.

A little more than an hour later I had passed the *Modernaire Motel* and left York behind me. I was now traveling along the 462, which would join with the 30 somewhere close to the end of my day. I was also already bathed in sweat at 10am. The Pennsylvanians following my journey hadn't been joking when they said it would get hotter each day now, and I wondered how much heat I'd be able to take, walking 30 miles a day...

A few hours in I was in bad shape. I drank as much as I could, but the heat was relentless punishment. And though my achilles tendon was doing okay I struggled with the pain in my feet. They were just generally hurting. If felt like there was a lot of pressure on them from every angle, like they were stuck in a medieval boot. And there was that stinging pain in the ball of my large left toe again. It seemed to get worse with every passing hour... Then, as I trudged along, somehow convincing myself that I would make it if I only kept it to a step at a time, I suddenly found myself on a massively long stone bridge. I stopped, surprised at its appearance. Its length was so extensive I could hardly make out the other end. It was old, with significant history, no doubt. It somehow didn't seem to belong here in rural Pennsylvania. 'What is this place?' I silently wondered, as my eyes drifted to the mile-wide riverbed below. There was a strange and intriguing feel to it, like all of a sudden I was transported to another country, or even another time. Maybe it reminded me of Europe, I'm not sure. I couldn't capture the dimensions, unfortunately, but this is it:

The *Veterans Memorial Bridge* connects the towns of Wrightsville and Columbia, which sit on opposite shores of the Susquehanna River, and was built in 1814 by Quaker and

207

Engineer John Wright. Near the bridge was located the first important Ferry over the Susquehanna River Gateway for Emigration into the Great West. As much as this structure's history intrigued me, I enjoyed the refreshing air coming off the river more than anything. I kept my face turned to the water as I kept walking, trying to capture any coolness and moisture coming off it, relishing the breeze like a spa-on-the-go treat.

Hours later, the welcome distraction of the unusual sight had faded to memory, and this day turned more brutal by the minute. It didn't take long before the pain in my left foot forced me to my knees (figuratively), and onto my back (literally):

I thought sharing a post would help. I wanted to feel like someone out there knew how I was doing, so at least I didn't have to go through it alone. In my experience loneliness is generally the most bitter pill to swallow on a journey like this. It worsens anything else you struggle with by a tenfold...

I had to keep going. As much as my body told me not to. As much as lying in the shade on soft grass felt like the best thing in the world in that moment. As much as I didn't know where to dig, to find strength inside me...

I don't remember many details from the hours following, other than it was an ordeal. On almost every step there seemed to be a tiny knife ejecting into the joint behind my large toe. I tried any which way to shift my weight and avoid the pain, but without success.

After about 28 miles I passed the shopping malls and outlets of Lancaster, PA, and - for one of the only times on this trip - there were plenty of motels scattered along the path for the next few miles. It was reassuring to know that I could stop at any point now, but I needed to do at least 30 miles, and so I booked ahead at the *Scottish Inn* another 3 miles down the road.

I don't know if I would have made it without Kimberly...

Kimberly and I had been communicating via Facebook for a few days now. She was a fervent Bernie Sanders supporter from Virginia, and was on her way to Philadelphia. She said she would love it if our paths could cross somehow, and so we shared our routes and I asked her to keep me posted on her progress. Now, with a little less than an hour and half to go, I received a message that she was closing in on Lancaster, and a few minutes later her white van with tag 'HORSUZ' (she has horses) pulled into the mall parking lot I was waiting at.

It was an awkward but joyous first meeting. I told her I was filthy, but we hugged anyway. It took me a few minutes to drop my mode and my defenses. I was in a lot of pain, and I felt like if I spent too much time getting comfortable talking, I would later regret it and not be able to keep going. But then I relaxed, and accepted an invitation to sit and chat for twenty minutes over ice cream. Kimberly had been on the road the whole day, and I was very moved when she told me she had gone 4 hours out of her way to meet me. That's how much she supported what I was doing. Incredible! We had a great conversation about Bernie Sanders and shared some anecdotes about each other's lives. I was filled with gratitude for Kimberly's effort to provide some human company, and when I had to set out again I actually felt much stronger than before:

(Kimberly)

Kimberly and I would later connect on many occasions in Philadelphia, but for now it was another bitter-sweet goodbye with someone I felt connected with on a profound level, through our mutual support and love for Bernie Sanders.

210

I tackled the final hour of the day. I was tough, but not unbearable. After stocking up on energy bars and Gatorade at a close by gas station, I finally arrived at the *Scottish Inn*. The *Scottish Inn* (which had an Indian owner) was nicer than most of the other motels, and I would enjoy the comfort of a King-sized bed that night. After removing the tape from my legs, I was baffled at how blackened they were from walking alongside traffic all day:

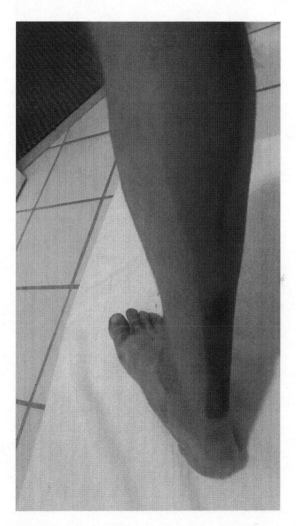

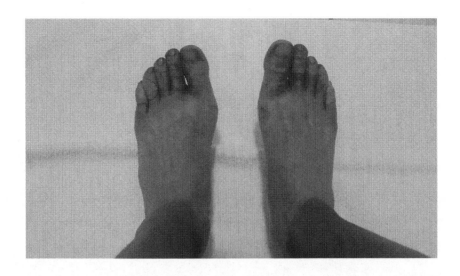

I took a bath, and washed the dirt off me. Afterwards, I removed my band aids to let my blisters breathe. My little toes, especially, still hurt a lot. The constant pressure had created callused red spots on top of each of them, that went deep into the tissue, and it would no doubt take a while for them to heal. The inside of my left heel was a similar story.

Having wrapped my knees and feet in ice, I laid back on the large bed and zapped through TV channels, consciously making an effort to enjoy the luxury. And somewhere deep below my fatigue and pain I felt an excitement growing: only two days left to Philly.

Day 24 - planned destination: Westchester, PA

I set out at 8:45am. I hadn't decided yet where exactly I would stay that night, but I knew I had to make it to the city of Westchester - a distance of about 34 miles. You know by now how much those long days took out of me, even without the heat. And, boy, was the air on fire that day: it wasn't even 9am yet and I was already dripping with sweat, incredulous it could be this hot.

Like any day since I had sustained my blisters, I spent the first stretch biting down on the throbbing pain coming from my toes. An hour, more or less, seemed to be the time it took until my body finally gave in on trying to make me stop, and a numbness set in, which was much more bearable. Both my achilles tendons were fine. The tape worked wonders, and it eased my mind not to have to think about it anymore.

I walked along the 30 for a while before Google maps told me to take a turn onto Strasburg Road. It looked like the rest of the day would lead me down a more quiet path, away from the traffic and the noise, which I was very happy about. It meant more shade and more grass. I remember distinctly how unbelievably hot it was, now that the temperature was peaking. I felt like a desert animal, trying to make it through the day without dying, dragging itself from water source to water source. I was functioning, nothing more.

Eventually I got more quiet and solitude than I had wished for - this was mostly rural farm land. When I stopped in the shade of a tree across a charming family home, slipping out from under my backpack and just collapsing in the grass, a man's voice called out to me. Sylvean, as I learned a moment later was his name, had seen me and was approaching the fence. 'Do you need some water?' he asked, apparently worried. I said that was very kind of him, and yes some water would be wonderful. He disappeared in the house and soon returned with some water and a large red apple. 'Here', he said. 'I thought you might like that, too.' I thanked him for his generosity. I saw that he had erected a small tent and a table in his garden, and he explained that he sold some produce from there as a little side business. I assume Sylvean was Amish, judging by his traditional haircut:

(Sylvean)

Like all Amish men and women I had crossed paths with on my walk, he was friendly, and evidently kind and generous. After a few minutes he said goodbye. We shook hands, he walked back inside, and I leaned against a tree and enjoyed the delicious apple. The water was wonderfully cold, and I soaked the bandana I wore around my neck - I had bought it at store earlier - with it. Soon the water would warm in the sweltering heat, but for now it was

Heaven on Earth.

I kept walking through quiet neighborhoods and past corn fields, with little traffic or other disturbances. And just when I thought this day would bring me to my knees with its uncompromising temperatures, I felt the first rain drops on my skin. Within minutes it was coming down in buckets, and I had to take cover under a tree to get a hold of Dave's rain poncho. I wasn't excited about getting my feet wet again - I remembered too well how that had worked out last time - but once I just accepted it, I actually had a blast. The air was so hot that the rain water was warm, and steam was rising off the road. It was like walking through a warm shower, and it even felt like the layer of water on the street provided some sort of cushion, softening the impact the concrete had on my feet. When the rain stopped and the sun reappeared behind the dark gray clouds, I walked over a bridge and saw an incredible view before me: the riverbed and the trees where veiled in white steam, and the golden sun illuminated everything like a magical scene from a movie. For a few seconds my mind stopped, and my pain and fears subsided. I didn't take a picture (probably because I had safely stored away my electronics in my backpack due to the rain) but the view was breathtaking...

A few hours later there were no traces left of the rain, and I had almost run out of water. Once again, there wasn't much opportunity around here for me to stock up on drinks and nutrition.

I noticed a family outside their home: a woman had just returned from grocery shopping, unloading the car, and a man - presumably her husband - had stopped mowing the lawn, to say goodbye to what must have been one of the couple's children with their partner. They were laughing, in good spirits, and they looked like openminded and openhearted people. 'Nothing to lose', I thought to myself, and walked over. I said hello, explained my situation, and asked if I could maybe fill up my hydration pack with water. A few minutes later we were standing on the porch together, I was holding gifts of crackers, chocolate, bananas and cheese, that Kelly (the woman) had brought me, and she and Arturo (her husband), who had filled up my hydration pack with delicious cold water, were listening to the story of my walk and the purpose behind it. I actually had to turn down a dinner invitation, because I didn't have more than a few minutes to spare:

(Kelly & Arturo)

I thanked Kelly and Arturo and headed out, once again nourished by strangers' kindness - and yummy cheese and chocolate.

Walking into the evening, the beauty of this part of Pennsylvania continued to put a spell on me. What I later learned to be Chester County was nothing short of spectacular. The trees and fields were lush and dark green, and the sounds of wildlife ever present:

It was the most *spiritual* part of my walk, for lack of a better word. I felt connected to a deeper state of being. Embedded in the fresh air and the underlying mysterious stillness of this place. As if the deepest essence of everything surrounding me was also my deepest essence...

The night came, as it always does. And I started to feel the already familiar symptoms, with several miles still to go. The heat had thoroughly worn me down throughout the day. My legs grew heavy. My mind was again reduced to dread and doubt. Would I be able to make it? Eventually I saw lights ahead, and I realized with great relief that I had reached Westchester. I had another mile and a half to go to my resting place, but at least it wouldn't be in complete darkness.

It was beautiful to walk through downtown, with its pretty lights and charming architecture. It was Saturday night, and Westchester was alive with people out on the town, having dinner or drinks. Students drove around in their cars with windows wide open, singing along to their favorite tunes, all of them enjoying life. It was here that I had my 'Into the Wild' moment I mentioned earlier. I felt so out of place walking past these nicely dressed people. I would have liked to join them. Experience the bliss of human company for a while. Laugh. Talk. Eat something nice, drink a beer or a margarita. Maybe even smoke a cigarette. But I didn't belong with the way I looked, the smell of dirt and sweat on me, and what I was out here doing. I was not part of society during this time... I was a traveler. Or a pilgrim. Or an activist of some sort. Maybe all of that. I still lived in Los Angeles, but the place I had called home for four years wasn't my home anymore. My relationship had ended, and my professional situation was as uncertain as ever. I was staying at my friend's apartment. In transition. In between things. My entire identity was blurry and undefined. And yet, in this moment - as much as I wanted to be part of 'normal life' again - all I could afford to think about was how to make it to my motel without seriously hurting myself. The ball of my left large toe was back and screaming bloody murder. The pain was intense, and the last mile a full out struggle.

I almost couldn't believe it when I finally walked through the doors of the *Microtel Inn & Suites*. The rooms were $120 a night, and this was the only somewhat affordable place in the area. Honestly, I would have paid three times the amount for some ice, a bathtub, and a bed.

When I got to my room I let in a bath and undressed. I saw my image in the mirror, noticing that I had kept losing weight. No surprise there. I unpacked my things and set my electronics up to charge for the night. I took the epsom salts I had left and poured them into the steaming water that was filling the tub. After this routine I took a pause, and sat down on the bed. I gave myself a moment to just be, and then the realization slowly but surely came to the surface...

I had made it to my last stop before Philly.

Day 25 - planned destination: Philadelphia, PA

It had taken me a while to fall asleep the prior night. The excitement of knowing I had only one day left had kept me awake. But I had gotten enough sleep to feel up to the task, and so - after a hot shower and a quick breakfast - I left the building with as much confidence in my step as I had ever had on this walk. I asked Google maps for my route, and soon looked at the phone with a big grin: exactly 27 miles left to go. I hadn't planned it. I had actually hoped for a much shorter last day, and with the *Microtel* being the only possible accommodation I had no influence on this whatsoever, but it was perfect.

Exiting the parking lot, I saw a car pull up on the side of the road. I was confused at first when I read the decal along the side of it: *Bino runs 4 Bernie*. And before I was able to put two and two together, I saw Michael Gibino step out of the back of the car. 'It's you!' I shouted with surprise and joy. I knew Michael had only been a half day or so behind me, and we had been trying to organize the logistics of meeting up. It was originally planned that he would overtake me much earlier on, but several injuries and other physical challenges kept delaying him. No surprise, considering this guy had been running one and a half marathons a day for a month to get to Philly (Michael has a marathon best of 2 hours and 45 minutes - a serious athlete - but this achievement is simply incredible)! We smiled at each other and hugged. I congratulated him on his monstrous undertaking, and he winked as he told me I hadn't done bad myself:

(Michael Gibino)

After meeting Michael's mother - she was driving the support car - and a friend of his, who had been running an entire leg with him the day prior, I was treated to some energy gels and bars out of the trunk. I saw that the car also served Michael as a place to take naps along the way, by simply putting down the seats. They had done it right. I chuckled about my own lack of preparation, and the subsequent obstacles and struggles. Michael told me he was going to get a few hours of sleep at the *Microtel* - he needed a real bed - before tackling the final 27 miles. 'Alright', I said. 'I'll see you in Philly.' And then I set out, waving as the Bino team made their way to the hotel.

I was deeply moved by our encounter. Michael and I knew essentially nothing about each other, and yet I could feel the bond between us. There was great power and relief in meeting the one person who really understood what the other had been through. And I'll never forget that Michael was out there at the same time I was, struggling, sweating, hurting, fighting... He's forever my fellow warrior for Bernie.

I walked through a short stretch of beautiful and quiet forest, with the occasional family home hidden away by the side of the road. The tree crowns let through flickers of sunlight, and walking in the shade like this was almost enjoyable. Then, for no reason whatsoever, sudden panic rose in my chest: what if I wasn't going to make it? What about the pain? What about the heat? What if my body just broke down and I couldn't recover? The fear was irrational, but I felt its power nonetheless. I simply told myself to keep walking, and was able to recognize that this probably happened because I was so close: it was the fear of finishing.

Soon I was heading down the 3 highway, which would be my route for the next 20 miles: one more time get through the monotony of walking for hours on the shoulder of a highway; one more time deal with the noise, the cars, the trucks and the motorcycles rushing past; one more time bite down on the pain and keep myself in the present moment. I hoped I could do it. 'One step at a time', I reminded myself.

Later - I was walking on a wide stretch of grass that some samaritan must have planted just for me - a car pulled up on the shoulder. I recognized the face of the young lady waving through the open window: it was Sarah, another Bernie supporter on her way to Philadelphia. We had tried to organize getting breakfast together that morning, but my schedule hadn't allowed it. I told her I would be walking along the 3, and that if she kept her eyes open for me, maybe we could meet. And here she was. We stood on the grass together for a few minutes, talking about what we expected to happen at the convention. How many people would come to protest? Could Bernie still be the nominee? Was there still hope?... We dared to believe it.

When it was time for me to head out again she told me to wait, and rushed to her car. She came back with an egg sandwich she had gotten at a restaurant earlier, and handed it to me. She told me she wanted to give me at least this to help me out, and I gladly accepted it. It looked delicious - *real* food! We hugged goodbye, she got in her car and we yelled the by now popular hashtag 'See you in Philly!' at each other, as she drove away. There was a warm feeling in my heart. It was the appreciation for this woman. For her support. For knowing we both fought for something meaningful:

(Sarah)

Not long after I was back to focusing on the road, and the heat intensified with every passing minute. It was getting close to noon, and the temperatures were sky high once again. My mind kept trying to trick me into anxiety and doubt. 'Just keep going', I interrupted that voice. 'One foot in front of the other. You've made it through worse on this trip. Just keep going.'

Striding past a shopping mall, a car honked at me from behind, and when it passed me I saw people were holding Bernie signs out the window. I waved back, surprised. I knew a lot of Bernie supporters would be heading into the city on this highway, but my Bernie shirt was only visible from the front. How did these people know I was a Bernie supporter before they even passed me? I found out a few minutes later... The car had stopped by the shopping mall, and now the family of four was heading my way on the cross walk. The parents (Sarah and Matt) had their little

222

daughters (Sophie and Bridget) by the hand, holding Bernie balloons and signs. They called out to me, seemingly excited to meet me: 'We've been following your journey! I'm so glad we get to meet you!' I was speechless - what a wonderful surprise. Sarah insisted on getting me a drink to cool down, and so we headed to the Starbucks in the mall, where I was treated to a giant Frapucino (I know I told you I hated working for Starbucks, but in that moment it was the best thing in the world). As always there was an inspiring conversation about Bernie. Sarah and Matt had the same clarity in their eyes that I saw in so many of Bernie's supporters. They understood. And despite the uphill battle, we were all still full of hope and vigor. Somehow it would happen. Somehow Bernie Sanders would be our next President. I enjoyed my time with them immensely. Sophie and Bridget were precious little girls, and all of them together just a beautiful family:

(Sarah and Matt with their daughters Sophie and Bridget)

Then I suddenly felt how comfortable I was getting, and I knew I had to go. I couldn't drop my defenses and my mode too much - they helped me deal with the pain - and the rest of the day would take everything out of me.

We walked to their car together, and hugged goodbye. I felt recharged by this family's generosity and spirit, and I walked on strengthened in body and mind.

Matt had told me I should be able to see Philadelphia's skyline soon, which excited me beyond belief. I knew once I could see the city with my own eyes, I wouldn't let go. And when it finally happened, it was glorious:

I was driven by knowing how close my final destination, the Wells Fargo Center, now was: less than 10 miles to go! At the same time I was hurting, felt worn down, raw and exhausted. Fear and doubt once again found their way into my thoughts. Who knew what it would be like to finish this walk? What would expect me once I got there? Would my friends Becca and John-Michael be there at my arrival? Would the anticipated crowds of Bernie supporters flock to the convention center, or would there be no one at all?

And so I walked through the first residential areas of the outskirts of Philadelphia, feeling all emotions at once, when I noticed something on the sidewalk right in front of my feet. I

224

stopped and squatted down, which hurt like Hell, but I didn't care: there was a tiny baby animal on the concrete. Its body was still warm, but it was lifeless. I had never seen anything like it, but I know now it was a baby possum. I picked the little fella up. His body was unspoiled. He had probably fallen off his mother's back. I put him on some leaves, and placed him on the wall next to the sidewalk:

And then I completely fell apart... Looking at this little creature, whose spark of life was irretrievably gone, the tragedy of life and death hit me with full force. I wished for nothing more than for him to come back. He had barely crossed over, and looked like he could wake up again any second. In that moment I couldn't accept that he had expired. I don't know if anyone noticed the grown man bawling his eyes out on the side of the road, but I couldn't have cared less. After a few minutes I picked myself up and walked on, letting the scorching sun dry my tears...

Soon the convention center was only 5 miles away. I began to feel the fatigue. The never ceasing pain was like a grinding wheel to my psyche, and the overall effort of this month-long undertaking made itself known loudly and clearly. But somewhere inside I knew that nothing would stop me now.

I decided to rest for a bit in a small park I passed. I laid down on my back, and put my feet up on a bench. The sunlight was playing with the leaves a few feet above me. It was beautiful to behold, and I tried to fully enjoy what I thought would be my final stop before my destination.

I went on, and soon broke the next barrier as the mile count went below 3, which meant less than an hour to go:

Shortly after I came through a poor and crumbling neighborhood. Once again, it was primarily African American, and in a tragic way it felt fitting: I had started my walk in the South of Chicago, where Bernie Sanders had been arrested for protesting segregated housing in 1963, and all these years later the area was still poor and crumbling. And now on the last miles, I passed through a similar area. I recorded a quick video and shared my thoughts on my page: justice isn't true justice when it doesn't cover every department. Racial justice, social justice, economic justice, criminal justice, environmental justice - they all are connected.

And Bernie Sanders understood that better than any other candidate, and maybe better than anyone in the US. That's why his platform covered all of it. He had built his campaign on the core principles of true equality and true justice for all, and on the promise of a future where everyone in this country, really *everyone* - no matter what color of skin, heritage, gender, religion, creed, sexual orientation - would get a fair shot at a good life. Nothing more. And certainly nothing less.

About forty minutes later the mile count fell below 1. My brain began to pump large doses of adrenaline through my body. I felt the rush in my blood and in my muscles, pushing me forward, accelerating my steps. I was so close now that I knew with absolute certainty that I was going to make it. Even if I had suddenly broken a leg, I would have dragged myself there.

Almost in trance I heard a car honk at me, as I passed an intersection. Bernie signs and writing on it were on full display. 'Hey, are you the guy who's walking here?' the man behind the wheel shouted through the window. 'Yes!' I yelled back with a big grin. 'I'm almost there!' The lady on the passenger seat gave me a thumbs up, and the two waved and honked as they drove on. These people had heard about my journey and recognized me - what an incredible feeling.

With half a mile to go I made my second to last turn, and was now heading along a fence adjacent to a park. I saw more and more Bernie T-shirts and other Bernie gear on people that passed me, and almost all the cars parked around here had Bernie bumper stickers on them. The final turn wasn't far now. I stopped by a park bench, and changed into the Bernie T-shirt Jeanne had given me back in Gettysburg. I wanted a picture of myself by the fence they had allegedly erected around the Wells Fargo Center, and my own light blue T-shirt was a mess, and almost completely faded from the sun. I put my backpack on one last time, took a deep breath, and willed my legs to carry me down the final stretch. 0.2 miles to go, maybe 0.3...

As soon as I turned the corner, I could see the police presence and the wide double fence around the convention center. There it was, my final destination. I could barely make it out in the distance, however, since the barrier created a perimeter of literally over a hundred yards. I wouldn't be able to get closer than the fence, but I had known that all along.

I was now only a few hundred feet away. I put my head down and my focus back on my next step. Close to the end or not, this *was* the last stretch of the day... Then I suddenly heard excited voices close by: a group of Bernie supporters, who were passing me, had stopped. One of the ladies looked at me with wide eyes. 'Are you the guy who's walking here?' she asked. 'Yeah', I gave back. 'I'm just coming in right now. Just gotta touch the fence and I'm done.' Her face lit up. 'Oh my God, you've been all over social media today', someone else said. 'You're posts keep showing up in my feed!' They all wanted to take a picture, and I couldn't have been happier to oblige. Though a part of me was extremely aware of how close to the end I was - literally two more minutes of walking - and yet I was standing on the sidewalk, talking to people. 'I can't drop my defenses', I knew. 'I'm not there yet.' More people joined, wondering what the ruckus was all about, and it turned out many had followed my walk online, or at least heard about it. Isn't it funny? I had had elaborate fantasies about this moment to keep myself going, and - while Bernie wasn't there, and Becca and John-Michael were filming interviews with Josh Fox and Nomiki Konst in Vernon Park for our documentary - I was actually granted a sort of hero's welcome:

It was beautiful. Rewarding. Touching. Inspiring. I loved these people for coming up to me, and for being in Philly to fight for a better future for everyone in this country.

Eventually, all the pictures were taken and all the words exchanged, and we said goodbye. Only one man and one woman stayed with me. They asked if they could film my last steps to the fence. 'Of course', I smiled. 'Let's go.' And so we walked the last two hundred feet. The man filmed me with his phone, simultaneously asking questions about the journey. He seemed excited about our meeting, and that made me happy.

And then I was there...

I stepped off the path, and onto the grass. The fence was now at arm's length. A man and a woman in police uniform were positioned stoically behind it, about 15 feet away. 'This is it', I told the man and the lady who were still with me. 'Once I put my hand on it, I'm done.' I looked through the wire to the Wells Fargo Center in the distance - the place where everything would be decided in the coming days - and reached out my hand, finally making contact. Nothing happened. No jolts of energy came shooting through my hand. No glorious feelings of triumph made my chest burst open. No emotions suddenly exploded to the surface and forced me to my knees. I just felt the rusty wire under my fingertips. I was here. It was done. Nothing more, and nothing less. If there were tears reserved for this moment, or a feeling of achievement, I had long shed them or felt it while imagining what the end would be like. All I knew was that I didn't have to walk anymore.

I asked the lady if she could take a picture of me. I needed to share with my Facebook followers that my walk was finished and, of course, I needed a memory. I wanted the picture to represent what this walk had been about, but I didn't know how to do that. Then I spontaneously remembered a photograph I had seen of Bernie Sanders: he had his fist raised, which showed his fighting spirit, but his humble expression also made it clear that he never forgot that this wasn't about him. It wasn't planned, and I didn't know how the picture would come out, but the sunlight hit the Bernie shirt just right, and left me more or less in the dark. I shared it on my page, together with this caption:

We made it to convention, guys. We're #StillSanders and we're still #NotMeUs. Thank you for carrying me.

This was for you.

I sat down to rest my body. I tried to just be there and to let it sink in - whatever needed to sink in.

Then I grabbed my phone, and ordered an Uber to bring me to Vernon Park. I wanted to see my friends. I longed for companionship, and then to head to the apartment we shared to take a hot shower and get something to eat. I smiled when I saw the comments and reactions to my post coming in faster than I could follow: thousands congratulated me and thanked me. It's hard to express in words what that felt like.

I arrived at Vernon Park. Bands were playing, poets rhyming and Bernie Sanders surrogates such as Danny Glover and Susan Sarandon speaking. People were dancing, singing, sitting in circles. It was a loving and warm atmosphere I walked into.

Becca welcomed me with a hug and a big smile and - since I had literally just arrived - we made use of the moment and did a quick interview. I tried to sum up my journey in a few words, and described how it felt to have made it to Philly. John-Michael gave me an enthusiastic hug before he returned to interviewing people for the documentary, and I just hung out and waited, enjoying not having to move. That's when I saw Ed Higgins: Ed had been one of the most fervent Bernie supporters and activists throughout the entire primary. We had never met in person, but we had been in contact via Facebook, since Ed led his own march in support of Bernie. We hugged, excited to finally meet, and shared some more stories about blisters and other bodily aches we had endured (as I'm writing this book Ed is out there at Standing Rock, protesting against the North Dakota pipeline. Together with many other brave activists he's fighting for our clean water and for the rights of the Native American tribes to be respected, putting himself in harm's way, as peaceful water protectors are maced, shot at, beaten and caged by the police, which acts as a private army for the big corporations invested in the pipeline. Thank you, Ed!).

After all the interviews were done, Becca, John-Michael and I were headed to our Airbnb and finally had time to chat over dinner. We talked about everything, from what kind of footage we needed for the documentary, to what our expectations were for the coming days:

(my fellow revolutionaries John-Michael & Becca)

Could Bernie still make it to the nomination in what was officially a contested convention? I think deep down we all knew that - considering the apparent corruption within the DNC, their rigidness, and their disregard for true democracy - Bernie Sanders wouldn't stand a chance. Yet, we still hoped.

<u>Philly</u>

The days following were filled with magnificent and beautiful experiences, as we took part in this historic event. We protested outside the convention center, banging on the fence, screaming our lungs out to be heard by the Clinton delegates who walked past under police protection:

There was no violence. There wasn't even any conflict. The thousands of people who had come here to make themselves heard, and to protest against a corrupt system that had ignored their voices throughout the entire primary cycle, were nothing short of inspiring. The boundless love, the instantaneous connection, and the deep understanding between all these supporters of Bernie Sanders - all of which was based on the very values this Senator from Vermont had reminded us of, as he spoke of compassion and caring for the least among us, time and time again - was deeply moving, and I will never forget being among these great people during those days in Philadelphia. Among them were Jeremy White, a badass activist and organizer for the Bernie movement back in LA, Jessica Salans, an inspiring young woman who I had met just months prior, and who is running for city council for LA's 13th district as I'm writing this book, Tim Black, a writer and online show host who had given me a shout-out on his page, Mikki Willis, a filmmaker and activist who interviewed me about my walk, Claudia Stauber, an author and activist who had been a powerhouse of support for Bernie throughout the primary, and many more... Every one of them who was out there fighting with the weapons they had at their disposal - their voice, their anger, their care, their outrage, their hope - are heroes to me. And so are Bernie's delegates, who were fighting for us inside the convention center, as they were disrespected, endured unprecedented obstruction and ridiculous last-minute rule changes, verbal attacks and all kinds of other shenanigans at the hands of the Clinton campaign and Democratic party members. And, speaking of heroes, two names in particular must be mentioned here: former Ohio State Senator Nina Turner and Hawaii Representative Tulsi Gabbard stood by their full-fledged support for Bernie Sanders throughout the entire primary, despite threats from within their own party, despite being painted as non-feminists for not endorsing Hillary Clinton, and despite risking their political future. Their integrity, their courage, their intelligence, their compassion and their uncompromising belief in true democracy were and are truly awe-inspiring, and I hope with all my heart that *they* are the women girls will look up to and model themselves after in the years to come. Not the Hillary Clintons of this world. Not the Debbie Wasserman-Schultzs. Not the Donna Braziles... Not those who cheated the country out of a fair election.

My own personal highlights during my time in Philly have to be the many encounters I had with people who had been following my journey. Every day I was recognized wherever I went. People hugged me and thanked me. We took pictures, and talked. Every single one of those meetings was special, and I felt humbled to have had these people's support.

One encounter stood out, even among all the others: a man and a woman with their two children - a girl of about 4, and a boy of about 2 - came up to me as I was sitting down somewhere outside FDR park. We said hello and, as always, I was delighted to meet perfect strangers, who knew what I had been doing. They told me how they had been so numb to politics for their entire adult lives, and how Bernie Sanders had shaken them out of their sleep. And now they couldn't not fight for their children's future, and they thought it was important to bring them here. It was a powerful statement, and I couldn't agree more. Their eyes were sparkling with clarity. 'Thank you for sharing that', I said. 'And for coming up to me. It means a lot.' We took a picture together, and as we went on to say goodbye, the lady looked at her little daughter. 'Can you say thank you to Bernhard?' she asked her. The girl looked at me, a little confused, and then back at her Mom. 'Why?' she asked. 'Because he walked a really long way here', the mother replied. 'To take a stand. And he did that for us.' The girl smiled at me and said: 'Thank you.'

I struggled to hide the emotions bubbling up inside me, as we all wished each other the best and said goodbye...

He did that for us.

I had had a faint hope that I might be able to give something to other Bernie supporters through my walk. I knew they all had been holding on for dear life throughout the madness that was this primary, and when I heard those words I knew that - at least for some of them - I had. I cannot tell you what that means to me.

And more importantly, those words encapsulate the work and life of Bernie Sanders: he did all of what he did *for us*. Unlike the Cintons and the Trumps of this world, Bernie Sanders didn't care

236

much about his own status, personal wealth or fame, about being Congressman, or Senator, or President. He cared about the people. And whatever he needed to do to help the American people, *that's* what he would do. And that's what he had done throughout his entire political career, and even before that when he was standing up for civil rights as a young student in Chicago. And all the hours and the near-superhuman effort he had put into his speeches and interviews and debates and fundraising, and whatever else he had done throughout his 2016 campaign - he had done that for us. As far as the convention is concerned, you know the outcome. I highly recommend to check out John-Michael's and Becca's documentary 'The Trouble With Normal.' It will give a vivid insight into what went down in and around the Wells Fargo Center during those four days...

The Way Back

On Thursday, July 28th, everything had already been decided, and I had to make my way back to the West Coast. A fellow Bernie supporter from Buffalo, NY - her name was Melissa - offered to drive me back to Chicago. She was a professor for language, and since she was off for the summer she didn't mind taking the trip. It was her way of showing her support, and I was very grateful for her generosity. She picked me up that day, and off we went:

(Melissa)

It's potentially challenging to spend a whole day in a car with a perfect stranger - Philadelphia to Chicago isn't exactly a short trip - but Melissa and I had a great time, and lots and lots to talk and rant about. Like with others who had helped me along the way, there was an unspoken trust due to our love and support for Bernie Sanders, and we knew we shared the same values.

It was a peculiar experience to cross the distance I had walked and scooted over the course of 25 days in less than 12 hours. But that's how long it took us until we arrived at the Damato house in Elmhurst, just outside Chicago. Melissa said she would find a motel close by, and then head back to Buffalo in the morning. I thanked her, which felt inadequate for what she had done for me. We hugged, promising we'd let each other know that we made it home safely. Then we said goodbye.

I slowly walked down the driveway. I smiled as I laid eyes on my Jeep again. There it was, my trusty old companion, the tarp covering it still firmly tied down:

I made my way up the stairs. 'Dave? Wanda?' I called out tentatively. Before I reached the door I already heard Dave's smoky voice: 'Bernhard, you made it!' Once again, I was welcomed with open arms by the whole family. They fed me and made me feel at home. We talked for a while about everything that had happened, and mourned the outcome of the convention. After telling Dave how invaluable his orange rain poncho had been on my journey, I went to bed. I slept like a baby that night.

The next day I realized that the puddle on top of my Jeep had seeped through the tarp, and the floor of the car was completely under water. After Dave and Jeremy helped me scoop out the water, they invited me along for a hearty and delicious breakfast at a diner close by, to provide some strength for the long car journey ahead (I had said goodbye to Wanda the evening prior - she had to go to work early in the morning):

(Dave & Jeremy Damato)

Then Dave had to leave for his shift at the toll both he was working at. 'We might see each other when you pass through later', he informed me. 'It's on your way.' Then he handed me a little bit of money for the journey. 'It's not much', he said. 'But please take it.' I was very moved. I knew the Damato's weren't swimming in money, but I accepted. I felt it was Dave's way of expressing a sort of fatherly care for me. Somehow we had bonded in the short time we had spent together. 'I'll be either at the rightmost booth, or the one next to it!' he called out, as he jumped in his car and drove off.

A little later Jeremy and I were about to say goodbye, when another obstacle presented itself: the battery on my Jeep was dead as doornails. Lucky for me there was a mechanic right around the corner who quickly replaced it, and within a little more than an hour I was ready to head West once again. I thanked Jeremy for his family's hospitality, then we hugged goodbye.

I loaded my things into the Jeep, got in and started the engine. *Wrooom*. 'I love this car', I thought to myself. It was 27 years old, had 146,000 miles on the meter, and it had taken me all the way from LA to Chicago without any issues a month prior. I was looking forward to being on the road together for the next three days. 'California, here we come!'

After a few miles I saw the first toll booths coming up. I remembered what Dave had told me, and I decided to go for the rightmost lane. As I closed in, I could already see him in his neon yellow work jacket, waving. I stopped the car and we quickly shook hands. Then he opened the barrier (of course, he didn't charge me). 'Take care of yourself, buddy', he said. 'Thank you for everything Dave', I responded. Then I stepped on the gas, waving my arm out the window, and feeling a ton of gratitude in my heart.

Due to my delayed start, I only made it as far as De Moines, IA, on the first day.

On the second day, shortly after coming through Lincoln, NE - I had just stopped at a gas station to fill up my tank, and get some food and drinks for the road - I saw a hitchhiker on the shoulder of the ramp getting back on the 80 highway. For a second I felt the urge to stop, but then kept going. I didn't want to get involved.

'You shouldn't pick up hitchhikers', the voice of reason in my head agreed. Then I remembered how desperate I had been that night in the middle of rural Pennsylvania, and how much I would have appreciated someone to stop for me... I stepped on the breaks, and pulled over.

The hitchhiker had taken notice, I could see him pick up his bags and make his way toward me in the rearview mirror. He was short and stocky. His bald head was covered with a baseball cap, and his eyes hidden behind sunglasses. He stuffed his things in the back of the Jeep before he had even acknowledged me, or spoken a word. Somehow I had expected gratitude or at least politeness, and a part of me immediately regretted my decision. 'How's it going?' I asked. 'Much better now', he said as he got in the car. He still had his shades on and it left me unsettled. I wanted to see his eyes. I wanted to know who I was dealing with, if I was going to drive this person to who knew where. 'I'm Bernhard', I introduced myself. 'Mike', he responded, and shook my hand.

I started the car and steered it onto the highway. 'How far am I taking you, Mike?' I inquired. 'About 150 miles', he responded. He seemed curt and closed off. Not particularly interested in having a conversation, apparently. And now I would have to deal with this mysterious stranger for the next two hours... Great. 'Was this a smart thing to do?' I thought to myself, trying to keep an eye on him.

After a few minutes I gave it another go: 'Do you live where I picked you up? What's the reason you're hitching a ride?' I asked. 'Yeah, I used to live here', he answered. 'But my wife died two weeks ago. Now there's nothing left here for me.' I felt like I got sucker punched. 'Oh my God', I'm sorry to hear that, I said. 'How long were you married for?' He said that he had moved here for her from Huntington Beach in California 26 years ago, that she had been the love of his life, and that she had been sick for a long time...

Jesus Christ. I crumbled inside. The poor guy. No wonder he kept his shades on and was sparse with words. I could feel the

242

sadness pouring out of him like thick fog. From the side I could see his eyes shimmering behind the glasses. I shared with him that I had been devastated when my fiancee and I had recently broken up after four and a half years, and I couldn't fathom losing a partner of 26. He acknowledged it with a bitter nod. And so we drove along, Mike and I, two heartbroken men with no idea what life had in store for us next, and not much else to hold on to in that moment than each other's quiet company.

A couple of hours later I dropped Mike off in the city of North Platte, NE. He was going there to work. He was a painter. 'It's tough losing the person you love and that knows you best', he told me, after he had unloaded his things from the car. 'I've never felt this lost and alone in my life. I don't know what's going to happen.' Sometimes there are no words. What can you say to someone who's had his life torn in half, and forever lost a part of himself? I shook his hand, trying to somehow communicate to him that I appreciated the time we had had, and said goodbye.

When I was back alone on the road I cried. I was still so raw from everything I had gone through, and the depth of grief this man had to endure left me completely defenseless. And so the drive through the rest of Nebraska was still and mournful. I pondered my own situation. Now that I was returning to LA, I would have to pick up my life again. And I didn't know what it would look like. So much had changed on many levels...

The sun was on its downturn when I entered Colorado, and it wasn't long before it got dark. I had been continuously driving uphill for a while now, and it was getting chilly. And then it suddenly hit me: 'I'm in the Rocky Mountains!' On my way from LA to Chicago I had taken a more Southern route, since the original starting point for my walk was going to be St. Louis. But now I was on the 80 heading back to California, and I completely forgot I'd be coming through here. And so higher and higher I went. 9,000 feet, 10,000 feet... As I kept driving - speaking silent prayers that the Jeep wouldn't break down on one of these narrow uphill roads in complete darkness - I began to wrap myself into whatever pieces of clothing I was able to fish out of my backpack. I was not prepared for the cold and I was still in shorts and T-shirt. So another T-shirt became a scarf, the sun hat a wind hat, and the windbreaker - well, remained a windbreaker. When I crossed the highest pass at 12,000 feet around 9pm, I was grateful for every piece of fabric I had on me:

Then - it was thankfully getting warmer again, since I was once more on the descent - I heard a very unsettling noise coming from the engine... I was on a short uphill stretch when the car began to stutter, and I suddenly wasn't getting any response from the gas pedal. I quickly shifted back in gear, hoping it would help the Jeep find its grip again, but it didn't. It sounded like the engine would die any second. I knew I had enough gas, and whatever this was had never happened to me before, so naturally I was worried. Let's say *terrified:* I was in the Rocky Mountains, in the middle of the night, with an old Jeep that could be seriously damaged, for all I knew.

I don't know who looked over me, but I somehow made it to a gas station on a hill about a half a mile away. Every worry in the world ran through my head. This had to be bad. And I was broke as never before. I wouldn't be able to pay for any substantial repair. I tried to stay calm. I got some water and a snack at the store, before returning to the car, hoping that the problem would magically disappear while I was gone. 'Is there any way I don't have any gas left?' I thought to myself. I decided to fill up, just in case, and that's when something occurred to me: the last gas station I had filled my tank at sold not only the usual 87, 89, and 91 octane gas, but also 85. In most states such a low octane rating isn't available. I had chosen it, since it was the cheapest gas, not considering that it might give the Jeep trouble. Now I realized that with the constant uphill driving, the low quality of the fuel could have had an impact on its performance. I put my theory to the test and filled the tank with 91 octane gas. And sure enough: the car started fine, the stuttering was gone, and I didn't have any troubles for the rest of the way. Phew. You live and you learn. I can't tell you the relief I felt.

The night was getting long. I had decided to stay in Glenwood Springs, CO, and I was completely exhausted when I finally got there a little after midnight - 824 miles since setting out from Des Moines. There were tons of motels and hotels in Glenwood Springs, and so I hadn't thought it necessary to call ahead to reserve a room. I approached the reception of the motel I had picked, and asked for a room for one night. 'We're all booked out', the lady said. 'And I'm afraid you won't find any vacancies in town tonight', she added. 'Dear God, no', I thought. 'I can't keep driving. I'm too tired.' I called a few of the hotels and motels, and the lady was right: everything was booked out. It was summer, school was still out, and this was apparently a popular vacation spot. So, not too big of a surprise, really. I called other places in the area, and the closest motel I could find that had rooms available was in Grand Junction, CO, 86 miles away. I had been driving for 14 hours. I didn't have another hour and a half behind the wheel in me. Not this late at night. But what choice did I have? I ate an abysmal bean & cheese burrito I had bought at a gas station, mentally preparing myself, and then I headed out.

By the time I reached the *Days Inn* in Grand Junction, I was a complete wreck. I don't know how I was able to stay awake for the last miles. To top it off, I had to spend almost half an hour at the front desk, because all of my credit cards were declined. I found out the next day, that Bank of America had suspended them because my purchases going cross country were suspicious to their fraud detection system. Funny, because doing the same thing a month earlier hadn't been a problem... I was close to a mental breakdown. The poor lady at the front desk must have noticed, because she said I could just pay in the morning, once the card issues with the bank had been resolved. I expressed my heartfelt gratitude, and apologized for my grumpy mood. She smiled, and said she understood.

I was asleep as soon as my head hit the pillow.

Thanks to the extra 86 miles I had put in the night before, my final day was going to be a little shorter: 775 miles. Doable.

It was getting hotter and hotter now the further South I was driving. I stopped for lunch at a restaurant in Beaver, UT. I had frequently checked social media during my breaks along the way, and I had seen more and more posts popping up, where Hillary Clinton supporters expressed outrage at the Bernie Sanders crowd that vowed to not vote for her under any circumstances, due to the fact that her campaign and the Democratic Party had rigged the election, and in effect cheated Senator Sanders out of the nomination. The general consensus among them now seemed to be, that these Bernie Sanders supporters would be to blame should Donald Trump, the Republican nominee, win the presidency. I had had a lot of time to think out there on the road, and built up a considerable amount of anger in regards to this ridiculous notion. As I was waiting for my food, I recorded a video, adding my two cents to the discussion. I spoke to those people and told them that it was their responsibility we were left with Hillary Clinton and Donald Trump, not ours. After all, *they* had voted for her. *They* had chosen to completely ignore the many

246

polls that showed her losing to Trump, while Bernie Sanders was beating him by huge margins every time. *They* had disregarded her abysmal favorability ratings, and arrogantly dismissed the fact, that she was under criminal investigation by the FBI, for both her private email server and possible corruption regarding donations made to the Clinton Foundation during her time as Secretary of State.

My video struck a chord. Within 72 hours it got shared over a thousand times, and seen by over 100,000 people.

Meanwhile I had the rest of Utah, Nevada and California still ahead of me. As I mentioned before, it got hotter and hotter the further South I drove, and there's a fun fact worth mentioning: it was 8pm and already dark when I came through Baker, CA, about 90 miles South-West of Las Vegas. There was a long line of standstill traffic, and as my Jeep rolled to a stop I noticed the unbelievable heat. Baker is in a long-stretched, wide valley, which must be how the heat gathers and sits there like an invisible carpet. Most people around me had their windows up, and their ACs on. So I was the only one looking around in disbelief, eager to share with someone else how remarkable and otherworldly this felt. It was night, we were in the dark, and I was dripping with sweat. I checked the temperature on my phone: it was 108 degrees Fahrenheit.

During the last hours on the road, I thought once again about all the wonderful people I had met on my journey. Most of them I told you about already, but there were many smaller encounters I'll always cherish: like the truck driver, who helped me push the Jeep to the gas nozzle when it had abruptly died, and the engine wouldn't start up. He had smiled at me as we shook hands, and said: 'I won't hold it against you', pointing at the Bernie sign on my car. Only then I saw he wore a Trump T-shirt... Or the lady, who squatted down next to me during a break outside a gas station in Greensburg, PA, to ask if I was okay, and - after hearing about my quest - went on to buy me a Gatorade, despite not giving a damn about the presidential race and clearly not being made of money herself... Or the woman at a gas station outside Findlay, OH, who gave me free ice for cooling my legs, so I didn't have to pay for a whole bag...

Not one person I encountered on my entire walk insulted or belittled me for what I was doing, though I would have been an easy target, displaying my convictions openly on my chest for everyone to see. No one even made a negative remark. Not the Trump supporters. Not the Clinton supporters. Not the Republicans. Not the Democrats. Not a *single* one. You want to know what's wrong with this country? It's not the people, I can tell you that.

Just before midnight I merged onto the 110 Freeway, and a few minutes later the Los Angeles skyline presented itself to me in all its glory. 'LA, I'm back!' I shouted into the night with euphoria.

I stopped by John-Michael's and Becca's apartment. They had already returned to Los Angeles via plane a day earlier, and I needed to pick up the key to our mutual friend Luke's house - his entire family was still in Pittsburgh, to take care of his Dad - where I had left all my stuff, and had temporarily stayed before heading out on my journey. John-Michael and I talked a little bit about everything we had experienced. We had been through something extraordinary together, and there was so much to process. Then we said goodnight, and I took on the last miles.

After twenty more minutes I finally arrived at Luke's house. I parked the Jeep. I had made it back.

The next day I went to see my friends Ian, Mike and Rodrigo. I wanted to thank them for everything they had done to support my walk and - most of all - I just wanted to be in their company again. It had been a lonely trip, this walk in support of Bernie Sanders.

I was welcomed back by smiling faces and embraced tightly. Ian actually recoiled when he hugged me, shocked at how much weight I had lost. For a while we just stood there. So much had happened since we had last been together, planning and prepping my walk more than 5 weeks prior...

One of the things I found out there is a whole other level of appreciation for family and friends. You don't *really* understand how precious a part of your life they are, until you're somewhere far away, alone, cut off and hurting. That's when you know how much you love the people who love you.

'You have to write all this down', Ian insisted. I looked at him, baffled. I had never even considered doing anything of that sort, and I wrestled with the decision for several days. It's a lot of work writing a book, I knew that, even if I had never done it before. Eventually, I decided to do it, because I understood that people need to document what happened during the 2016 primary. We need to share our experiences and insights, so those who come after us know that hundreds of thousands of us gave their all, fighting for a new status quo, to bring back compassion and humanity to the US political system, which has become a feeding ground for capitalistic predators. And I wanted to do it as a memory and a thank you to all those who supported me along the way, and - last, but not least - as a tribute to the man who wrote history in the year 2016:

Senator Bernie Sanders.

What Bernie Sanders understands more than any politician in the US, and what he awoke millions of us to, is that - as far as Government is concerned - no path is worth pursuing if it's not guided by compassion and by aiming to take care of every man, woman and child... *By taking care of each other.*

Thank you, Senator. And Bernie on!

"In my view, you judge a country not by the number of millionaires or billionaires it produces, but how it treats its most vulnerable people."

- Bernie Sanders

Acknowledgements

To Ian Duncan, Michael Wallace and Rodrigo Villacorta, who - other forms of support aside - gave a big chunk of their money to make this walk possible: you guys are the best, and I love you.

Many 'celebrities' refrained from making public their support for Bernie Sanders, in fear of consequences should he not win the nomination, which tells you a lot about the other candidate and what kind of democracy we live in. Still, many stood up for what they believed in. Here are some of them: Susan Sarandon, Mark Ruffalo, Rosario Dawson, Shailene Woodley, Dr. Cornel West, Shaun King, Nomiki Konst, Josh Fox, Harry Belafonte, Spike Lee, Danny DeVito, Danny Glover, Dick Van Dyke, Killer Mike, Red Hot Chili Peppers, Emily Ratajkowski, Viggo Mortensen, Margaret Cho, Adam McKay, Lil B - thank you for your courage.

Thank you to independent media and journalists: Wikileaks, We are the Media, Tim Black, H.A. Goodman, Jordan Chariton, Democracy Now, The Jimmy Dore Show, Real Progressives, Sane Progressive, and so many more - your work is invaluable.

Thank you to those who supported me financially during my walk: Rachel Dagdagan, Farrakhan Kabiri, Laura Hockenberry, Melissa Fiori, Ryan Casey, Kaytee Smith, Sashim Gardner, Jeanne Marshall, Charis Lynn Curtis, Rebecca Peres, Sabrina Defay, Sandra Vanasse, Kathleen Obrien, Charlotte Rodriguez, Michelle Mcclure, Dave Damato - every dollar mattered.

In addition, I want to thank all who supported me in any way, and especially on my page *Bernie for Bernie* - you guys got me through this ordeal.

And most importantly, I want to thank my family: my Mom, my Dad, my sisters Verena and Julia, and my larger family, who have always been there for me - I love you all.

Made in the USA
San Bernardino, CA
21 May 2017